P9-BZE-613

Feed the Need:

Teen Edition

DR. BRIDGET COOPER

Copyright © 2014 Dr. Bridget Cooper

Cover art by Dr. Bridget Cooper. Cover design by Kelly Gineo.

All rights reserved.

ISBN-13: 978-0692353042
ISBN-10: 0692353046

DEDICATION

This book is dedicated to the girls who keep reminding
and teaching me what it's like to be a teenager:
my extraordinary daughters, Jessica and Elena.
Thank you for being my inspiration.

2018
Hold your power ♡
JB

CONTENTS

TRIBUTES

"If you have good thoughts, they will shine out of your face like sunbeams and you will always look lovely." ·· Roald Dahl

I'm a huge believer in serendipity; in being at the right place at the right time. I have witnessed things coming together in almost magical ways and the only thing that these instances have in common is my willingness to go with the flow and follow the Universe's lead. And this is how this book came to fruition. I was presenting on conflict and communication to a group in a lovely little town in Southern Connecticut and there were some teenagers in attendance. These young people were engaged and attentive and asked questions to get the answers they were seeking. One of them, Kate, even asked me if I had a teen edition of my book, "Feed The Need?" It was like a smack right upside the head. Right there and then I just *knew* I had to adapt the book for a teen audience.

Some of you might think that I decided to write the teen edition for a profit motive, you know, to make some cold, hard cash. Nothing could be further from the truth. There's not a lot of money in book sales, especially when you self-publish. My true purpose is a lot more altruistic and has a heap ton of passion behind it. I had a rough path through my teenage years and I felt lost and hopeless during much of it. I've made a good life for myself and my kids since then, but it was a tough road. The thought occurred to me that if I could write and distribute a book that could guide teenagers so that they could avoid some of the destructive patterns that I developed in trying to survive my teens, I'd sleep better at night. I want to give tools to you that will make a significant difference in your life, tools that took me until my late 30s to define. If I can save you some time and heartache that will make me *so* happy.

Thank you for bringing your pain and curiosity to me and allowing me to have a part of your journey. I trust that you will be better for it, and I will be forever grateful for the chance to change your live for the better.

To my brilliant and beautiful teen and pre-teen daughters, Jessica & Elena: Now I've gone and done it. I've written a book that your peers will be reading! That might just be one of the most embarrassing things you could imagine happening, right?! Thank you for loving me anyway and for appreciating my purpose in all of this isn't to make you crazy but to make the world a better place for you. Thank you for enlightening me each and every day, I really do love you madly and without end. You are destined for true greatness and I'm blessed to share in your journey.

To Jayleen, Elijah, Maya, Robin, Abbey, Michele, and Sarah (and the rest of the UConn Club): Thank you for reminding me about what it means to be a teenager (and a pre-teen and a tween and a pre-tween) and sharing your joy and your struggles with me. I can't wait to see the adults you become.

To Joe: Do you know how to say anything but, "Of COURSE you can!?" You're such a powerful force in my life and I thank my lucky stars every day to have you walking beside me, cheering me on every step of the way. Your belief in me really does make all the difference. And let's not forget your amusement reading through my treasure trove of high school diaries and notes and keepsakes. Where were you when I was a teenager??? ☺

To my Accountability Team (Mike, Lisa, Deb, Thom, Joe, & Kim): Thank you for holding my feet to the fire and encouraging me to nail my list. I added this BHAG (Big, Hairy, Audacious Goal) late in the game so I appreciate you not letting me slide on the rest. One more book done…many more mountains to go!

To Kate Adriani: Thank you for the brilliant idea to write this book! Kismet really does happen and it occurred that auspicious night in Easton, CT. I admire your courage and your maturity and I am confident that these traits will serve you well in life. Thank you for writing such an honest, thoughtful foreword to this book. Lives will change because of you.

To my parents (Mom, Dad, & Stan): You have all now left this world and I pray that you are looking over me, seeing how much our short time together influenced me. Thank you for teaching me so much about life, love, and loss. You are woven through these pages. There was a great deal of pain on our shared path, and through that, I developed insights and compassion that has proven powerful in positively affecting the lives of others ever since. Thank you. Thank you for loving me as best you could and giving me challenges so that I could appreciate the easier times.

To the adults and friends who reached out to me along my adolescent journey: Without your compassion, love, insight, and support, I'd have had a much harder path to this point. You helped me to recognize that we really do influence the lives of others, positively or negatively, and we need to take good care of each other if our light is to shine brightly.

To the adults I've encountered over the years who have been outright mean to me and to others: You've showed me that bullying doesn't end on the playground or in the school hallways. Wherever there is insecurity and pain there is meanness and punishment. Your destructive behavior has strengthened my resolve to make young people stronger so that they can shine in the face of your darkness. I pray that you find your way to the light.

And to the peers and adults who bumped into me <u>hard</u> when I was a teenager, I hope time has healed your wounds like it's healed mine. I wasn't happy about the hurts then, but I appreciate them now because they made me a stronger, more compassionate person.

To you, the reader: I hope the stories I share make you laugh, think, feel, knowing that you are not alone in this crazy journey we call "life."

"When everything seems to be going against you,
remember that the airplane takes off against the wind,
not with it." ~ Henry Ford

FOREWORD

"Doubt yourself and you doubt everything you see.
Judge yourself and you see judges everywhere.
But if you listen to the sound of your own voice,
you can rise above doubt and judgment.
And you can see forever." ~ Nancy Lopez

I met Dr. Bridget Cooper at a Girl Scouts' function that my troop hosted in my community on Communication & Conflict. I was not overly thrilled to be going because it was on a Thursday night, which was cutting into Thursday night football. For anyone who doesn't know me, I am a *huge* sports fanatic. While I was listening to Dr. Cooper, many of her words started to resonate with me. Talking to her after the event, I asked if she had a book for teens. I thought that if the talk was helpful to me, I knew it could benefit other teens, as well.

Listening to her speak changed my life *forever*.

While writing this foreword, I asked a couple of my friends what they thought teens struggle with the most in everyday life. Overwhelmingly, they responded with "fitting in at school." There is that mold that you have to fit and if you do not you're going to be an outcast.

I know that because through about sixth grade I always felt like the outcast. I knew I was different from everyone else, especially in school. I am dyslexic but proud of my differences now. When I was in elementary and middle school, I always felt that I would be made fun of for reading slower and messing up while I read. It took me until freshman year in high school to be fully comfortable with myself. I always felt beneath everyone because of my learning disability. I know others view me as an outgoing, bright, and bubbly person but it took a *long* time to get myself to believe that.

Coming into my senior year of high school, I have become more outgoing and comfortable with whom I am. Reading "Feed the Need" and going to Dr. Cooper's talk made me feel more confident, which I haven't felt in a long time. I absolutely *loved* reading this book. I thought the chapter summaries and exercises helped me focus on ways to improve myself and my relationships immediately.

I *know* if you are having problems in school or your personal life, this book is the way to fix them. The one exercise that helps me in my everyday life is the K-Bubble. It is my own personal bubble where I keep my crazy and do not share it with anyone else. All you do is put the first letter of your name in front of the word bubble ("J-Bubble," "M-Bubble," "C-Bubble"). This is one of the easiest exercises to incorporate into your in daily routine. I use this all the time!

Just the other day, I was at Dunkin Donuts and a customer was going off about her sandwich not being made right. The manager stayed in her bubble, validated the customer's feelings, but did not let them affect her. She kept herself calm and did not get wrapped up in the customer's crazy…and she was definitely *crazy*!

Another thing I have learned is that I cannot control *everything*. Dr. Cooper teaches that you have three buckets of control. The smallest bucket is the one you control (YOUR emotional needs), the middle size is outside influences (which YOU decide to let into your world) and the largest bucket is everything else that you cannot control. I didn't believe this at first, but I understand it now. I have control issues where I think I can control every single minute of every day.

Dr. Cooper helped me to realize I have to let it go, relax, and have fun or as she says STOP, CENTER, and MOVE. You are only a kid once. My favorite quote from this entire book is "You don't hang up your crazy at the door when you go out into the world: You bring it all with you." It is definitely the truth with many people in today's society. We are all guilty of putting our crazy life out there for others to get sucked into. I have come to understand that my crazy is my crazy and no one else's and I take it with me wherever I go. After the talk and reading "Feed the Need," I know understand this concept.

Meeting Dr. Bridget Cooper has changed the way I look at life and especially how I react to situations even though I am only 17. It is easy to change your life with her book and her talks. She makes you re-evaluate your life and the way you are living it. If you let Dr. Cooper do her magic you will see changes that you never thought were possible, without feeling the pain.

Kathryn (Kate) Adriani,
12th Grade
Academy of Our Lady of Mercy, Lauralton Hall

1

PROLOGUE

> "Good habits formed in youth make all the difference."
> ~ Aristotle

Pretty good for an old, dead guy from a long time ago, huh? I'm not nearly as old (and I'm clearly not dead) but I'm not a teenager anymore. I was once, though. I was reminded of that earlier this year when my mom passed away and I was digging through her attic to help to sort out what to keep and what to toss. I found the <u>motherload</u> of my teenage memorabilia: A box filled with notes, letters, diaries, photos, and keepsakes from way back when. I lost nearly a weekend scouring through all of it, reflecting on what it felt like to have my life revolve around the latest crush, friendship drama, mean girl, upcoming party or test, and what craziness my parents were doling out.

Want to know what I realized? Life for me today isn't that much different. Sure, the players have changed. Now I have deadlines from clients instead of teachers. These days my kids are doling out the craziness (shhh…). I still experience heartbreak on the romance front, including breakups and even a divorce. And friendships are just as complicated, if not more so. Bullies are still causing trouble. The only difference is that my hormones aren't raging. Wait. Yes they are…it's called menopause! All kidding aside, the only thing that differentiates you and me is that I've walked a path like yours and have some perspective. And I'm on a mission: To save you some pain.

I assume you have some amount of conflict with one or both of your parents. Maybe it's major: Mom or Dad is either gone or too unhealthy to have a good relationship with you. Maybe it's "just" a nuisance: Mom or Dad just don't understand you or you have a list of things that they do that annoy you to death. Maybe it's somewhere in between those two spots. Maybe they just know exactly how to embarrass you and do it anyway and it drives you nuts. Any way you slice it, your parents aren't perfect yet you have to live and deal with them. This book is going to help you to not only survive that, but actually thrive in your situation. Do you want to end up like your parents? I know I didn't. Maybe your parents are awesome, but there are plenty of adults you've run across that are your worst "that could be me in 20 years" nightmare. This book can help you avoid being them someday.

I also assume that if you have one or more brothers or sisters you fight with them, too. Maybe a little, maybe a lot, but I don't know anyone who doesn't have some conflict with their siblings. You're living together, sharing scarce resources (bathrooms, bedrooms, parental attention, money, rides, etc.) and you know just how to upset one another because no one knows you better than they do. This book is going to help you make the best of your relationships with your siblings, no matter how annoying they may be.

I've met with a lot of teens and I hear endless stories about bullies and cliques, too. Whether it's being ignored at the bus stop by people who were your friends in elementary school, or being teased at school by the "popular" crowd, it's rough out there. It can feel lonely and hopeless. I know, I do. This book is going to help to strengthen you so that you don't break in the face of bullies or mean people.

If I'd had "me" (and this book) when I was a teenager my path would have been a whole lot sweeter and easier. I needed these insights, perspectives, and tools more than I can express. I struggled as a teenager...a LOT. I nearly crumbled (or exploded) under the pressures I felt. I suffered from paralyzingly low self-esteem that I hid behind a cheerleader (literally) and over-achiever front. I was in unhealthy and sometimes abusive relationships but I couldn't see any way out. I tried, and failed, doing damage to myself in the process.

I want to save you some of that agony. Those experiences made me stronger, they really did, so I don't want your life to be perfect and easy. Just *easier*. And I want you to realize that you really are in charge of more than you might think. Yeah, adults are in charge of a bunch of stuff in your life, it's true. But you have a ton of control, too. And you can influence things a <u>lot</u>, for the better or the worse. I'm going to teach you the difference between *control* and *influence* so you can stop knocking yourself out trying to change things that you need to let go of and focus on the stuff you can. And when to reach out for help. We all need it. The strongest among us request it often.

I'm not the perfect expert on everything in this book. I'm a work in progress just like everyone else. I'm just here sharing my many stories to offer the insight I've acquired along my road. Plus, I could analyze a blade of grass fifteen ways to Sunday so you should know that I've pondered things in this book for years and years and years.

Have you ever obsessed over a paper you had to submit? I give "obsession" a whole new meaning when it comes to what I write. Whether it's a big paper, this book, or even an email, I read and re-read it to the point of near craziness. I honestly have no clue why I keep reading them, but I can tell you that after a day or so of this "ruminating," I could tell them to you verbatim. So, the revelations in this book aren't fleeting thoughts. I've pondered them for years, and thoroughly tested them with a procession of clients, colleagues, and friends. Oh, and on myself, of course, since I'm my favorite guinea pig.

It's often said that life only makes sense in retrospect. When you're in the middle of something, it's difficult to get perspective. And, it's impossible to see how the lesson fits into the overall mosaic of your life. You can't see how the door that closed opened other doors that led to other closed and open doors that led you down a path that now gives your life meaning. It's a big, old game of dominoes: Move one and the whole line is adjusted.

When I look back over my life, it's been chock full of experiences, that's for sure. Some were beautiful and happy, and some were downright horrifying. Some bridged both places: With joy and pain. As I look ahead to the rest of my life here on this planet, I know that the future will be much like the past. I'll love some, hurt some, and learn a whole bunch if I'm so willing. I hope that at your tender age that you see the same for your unfolding path.

In this book, I'll share stories: Some are mine, some are from clients, some are from friends, and some are from virtual strangers. Some of mine I will claim as my own; others that are mine will be shielded in "Dear Abby" style... "I have a friend" so that my privacy – and that of the people in the story – is protected. The original version of this book (for "adults") isn't that much different than this edition. I was going to do a total rewrite but then I realized that you don't need me to "dumb it down" for you to use the tools I present. I did change some examples so they would be more relevant to your own experience, so you'd know that I "get" you. Please feel free to skip the "For Dating Teens" sections if you're not there yet. Hang onto the book so you can read those pieces when you *are*.

Throughout this book, my hope is that you will find occasion to smile, to laugh out loud, to reflect, get flustered, maybe even cry, but most of all, to see the inspiration in every minute of your life. If this book has increased those moments, then I will consider it a success. Remember: Growth involves struggle, but it's worth it. So...Enjoy!

"Change yourself and fortune will change with you."
~ *Portuguese Proverb*

2

SETTING THE STAGE

"If you don't know where you're going,
any road'll take you there."
~ George Harrison

Needs. We all have them. Some of us own them. Claim them. Make them known. Some of us refuse to acknowledge them. Pretend that they don't exist. Ignore them as they rear their ugly heads. And, boys, it's not just girls who deny their needs. You guys do it, too. You confuse "needs" with being "needy." Or confuse serving the needs of others with being made of steel. So you fail to claim your needs with clarity and peace of mind.

Many young women have been trained to ignore many or all of their own needs in order to live out some martyred existence, turning themselves into human pretzels to "take care" of other people. Other women, my diva friends, think your needs are more important than anyone else's and no matter what others do for you, you are still never satisfied. You're the emotional black hole of need.

Young men, traditionally, have been told that aside from a few basic physical needs, you can handle everything on your own. You've been supported in making demands for recognition, authority, and control. Women, on the other hand, tend to get rewarded for how we serve the needs of others. The more we give (and suffer) the more valued we are. Or so we think.

I lived a great chunk of my life feeling responsible for what others felt, to an extreme that drove me into despair, low self-worth, destructive relationships, and more drama than even Hollywood would enjoy. I refused to own up to my own needs. I denied them and just served others to my own detriment. It wasn't until I was on my way out of my marriage in my mid-30s that I took a full inventory of myself and changed my thinking. I came to terms with what denying my needs had done to me. I don't want you to wait that long so I'm giving you the gift of this book as a huge leg up. Pretty awesome, right?

So, what did I learn? I figured out that my needs are my needs to fill. Your needs are your needs to fill. If I'm upset about something, it's not your job to fix it. If you're upset about something, it's not my job to fix it. If I've done something to hurt you, I'm obligated to make amends. If you're just hurt, it's not my job to fix that for you. I can try to cheer you up, but if you stay sad, it's not my fault. It took me years to come to this conclusion, but once I took full responsibility for identifying, communicating, and feeding my own needs, life got better. So much better.

~Black Holes of Need~

You may have been in one or more of those exhausting relationships where they suck the very life force from you because they demand that you try to fix them and make them feel better all the time. Yet, no matter how hard you try, it's never enough. Their needs are never fed to fullness. You're expected to take care of yourself *and* them. They seem helpless without you. And no matter how much you give, they want more. They are the black hole of need. And if you sign up for this lovely dance, you're in for a world of misery.

Some of these folks you can spot a mile away. A classic example of this is the diva. Some of these lovely ladies will own that title like it is a badge of honor, something to rejoice in. It is not. It's an example of a neediness that is destructive and pathetic in the same breath, but veiled behind a façade of independence and conceit. People who are truly independent and confident don't need to overpower or control other people. Clique leaders (and members) usually fall into this category. They seem to have it all together and use their position to make other people feel badly about themselves, especially if those people decide not to follow the "rules" of the group. They are bullies in pretty clothes.

Now, don't get me wrong: I'm not talking about the girls who are confident, clear, and poised and who avoid being a victim in their lives. Who take charge of themselves and are not afraid to have a voice and a presence and make history. No, not those "divas."

I am speaking of the individuals who demand that other people are at their beck and call, serving them above all else. When they say "jump," you're already expected to be in the air. They place themselves in the center of every situation, telling you what you'd better do for them, regardless of if they give even an ounce of attention or assistance to you. Oh, they might be nice at times so that you cannot see the depths of their selfishness. They might even say all the "right" things to make you think that you've misjudged them. Yet, actions always speak louder than words. Always.

They are always quick to tell you what you "should" do, overbearing in their certainty that there is only one way to do anything: *their* way. This covers everything from how you cut your hair, the shoes you wear, who you should like, and the book you're reading. If you do something differently than their advice indicates, you're clearly an idiot. You serve them. You support their view of the world by doing their bidding and following their commandments. And you should act grateful for the honor. So why does it feel like you want to scream as they tell you yet another thing that you "should" do? Because deep down you recognize that you are serving their needs to the exclusion of your own. You are a servant. And this feels ugly.

If you're in a relationship with a person like this (yes, divas can be male, too), what are you getting out of it? What needs of yours are being shortchanged? How do you feel being second fiddle, if you're even noticed at all? Are you tired of being in the shadows, treated like your needs don't factor into the equation? Like you don't matter? This book is all about needs. It's about figuring out the needs that you have and that drive you, and owning your role in satisfying them.

It's also about being aware of what is driving other people and how you can use that knowledge to improve your relationships through healthier communication and "good" conflict. What drives other people? The very same thing that drives you and me: Getting needs satisfied. If you're hungry, you're going to seek out food until you stuff your face with it and your stomach stops growling. If you need validation, you're going to figure out a way to get some attention for whatever it is that you do or have endured. And, like the little kid who is misbehaving, if you need connection with others, you're going to behave in any way that will get others to notice you and pay attention to you, whether or not it's positive attention. Some people out there are literally screaming with their behavior just to be noticed, touched, and loved. And some will actually die trying.

So, how can this book help? I identify four core needs that seem to show up in just about every conflict and dysfunctional relationship I've ever seen. The four core needs are:

- Connection (and Presence)
- Control
- Validation
- Passion (and Purpose)

You might be thinking that there are more needs that I'm not listing out. That may be true, but after you've read the book and learned how to identify an unmet need, you'll likely find that every need can be linked back to one or more of these four core needs. If you're feeling invisible and ignored, you're probably needing **validation** and **connection**. If you're feeling angry and distrustful, you probably need **control**. If you're feeling nothing in particular at all, even to the point of depression, you're probably needing **passion**.

My mother always told me that there is a difference between needs and wants. If you don't get your needs met, you don't survive. Wants are "extras" that are nice to have but they aren't musts. And now that I have kids of my own, I tell my daughters, "we do our have-to's before we do our want-to's." This book is all about satisfying our needs (our "have to's") so we can survive, and thrive. Your wants are often so critical, so central to who you are that you are sure they are "needs." Pssst…then they probably are needs.

If you aren't meeting your needs, you're slowly destroying yourself. You are failing to live the life you were meant to live. The life you were meant to live is not a life of drudgery and pain. It's a life of joy and abundance, of growth and challenge, of bringing all of your unique gifts to the world. Do you really want to settle for less? Do you want to feel unfulfilled even one more day? Do you want a life full of stress and sadness or anger or just "blah?" If so, pass this book to the person seated on your left, go grab a hot fudge sundae, and order a fresh copy of this book when you get sick and tired of being sick and tired.

This book isn't just about you, either. It applies to every person in your world. Again, when you aren't getting your needs met, you're apt to behave in dysfunctional, destructive, and desperate ways. And so does everyone else. We're all on the same stage, together. Your job is to focus on knowing what your needs are, and work toward getting your needs met. It's the same for everyone. But here's the problem: Not everyone is reading this book. Not everyone is committed to doing a self-inventory and making meeting their own needs a top priority.

What does this mean for you (aside from the fact that you're awesome)? In your relationships you will be bumping into people who have needs that they can't even identify, let alone have a clue as to how to get them met, including your parents, siblings, friends, and romantic interests. If you want to be happy, you must be able to identify the unmet needs of other people and figure out a way to meet those needs as best you can. If not, you'll keep feeling like you're slamming your head into a brick wall every time you interact with others.

I get paid to help people change their lives. I can only change lives when offered the invitation, so walk with me and we can change yours. I'm human and I struggle just like you and I'm offering up parts of my story for you to learn from, so you'll know that you don't have to be perfect to be amazing. In fact, the very best we can strive for is to be perfectly imperfect.

Use this guidebook for yourself and share it with your friends. Making a monumental change in how you behave doesn't require a full makeover all at once. Instead, it takes a small change, done consistently and with passion. That one small change will encourage more small changes which translate into a larger change with lasting results.

Why read this book? You've got a million other things to do with your time so why would you devote time to this book? If you're perfectly happy and feel peaceful and at ease in all aspects of your life then, by all means, put this book down and go back to whatever else it was that you have going on. I've met hundreds of thousands of people and I haven't yet met <u>one</u> who feels that way. So, if you do, you're beyond unique and I'm in awe. On the other hand, if you're frustrated with some of your relationships with other people (friends, parents, irritating classmates, etc.) or your own self (low self-image, anxiety, moodiness, etc.), then this book is the cure for what ails you.

It's a simple cure, too, but it's going to take some work on your part to put it into action. By getting started on this today, you're going to have a handle on having a happy, peaceful life faster than your peers, and perhaps faster than even your parents. How great would *that* be? This book is going to help you to identify the needs that you have and figure out how to meet them. To feel satisfied and even like life is "too" good. To do the same for the people in your world without going insane in the process. This includes your entire social and school/activity life, too. As my dear friend Lisa says, you don't hang up your crazy at the front door: You bring it all with you.

Once you realize that feeding your needs is at the core of every layer of happiness, so many of your struggles will disappear. If your needs aren't getting fed, you're going to be a problem to someone. If someone else's needs aren't being met, they are likely to be a problem for you. Or they will exit your life. Want the good news? Once you get into this "identifying the need to feed" mindset, problems will present simultaneous solutions: Figure out the unmet need and feed it. Start every problem discussion with "what need is not being met that is leading to this problem?" "What is this person lacking that's causing this fight?" "What is really making this person upset?" Your life will become so much easier with that one, simple step. You'll stop listening to the "noise" and getting caught up in the details. Instead, you'll be listening at a deeper and more effective level.

We all have a different path through life and face different challenges along the way. Not all of you face bullying and threats of violence, but many of you have or will. Not all of you face confusion about your sexuality (who you like, how to manage your feelings, how to share your body and with whom), but most of you have or will. Not all of you face disruption at home (divorce, death, parents fighting), but many of you have or will. Not all of you will be enticed by drugs and alcohol, but most of you have or will. Not all of you have a distorted body image, but most of you (like adults) struggle at times feeling not pretty, handsome, thin, shapely, or strong enough. Not all of you will have a hard time fitting in and figuring out who you are and where you want to be, but most of you (like every adult I know) will have some of these confusing and painful moments.

It's a tough world in many ways, and adolescence is a time where you'll be faced with a lot of challenges for the first time, and you may not have a clear response. This book promises to get you in touch with your own motivations and patterns so you can get clear on how you can manage all of those challenges the best way possible. The challenges won't disappear: You'll just become more of an emotional and relationship ninja, more prepared for the things that come your way. Apply the lessons and the examples I offer to the things that challenge *you*, knowing that each person who reads this book may have a slightly different set of problems they are facing.

As you read this book, you'll find that I ask a lot of questions. I do this so that as you read you can check yourself against the lesson presented, and to see where you might need to entertain a few shifts in your thinking and behavior. I'm paid to ask questions to discover what you want and what is standing in your way of getting that. In my work as a leadership consultant and trainer, I ask, listen, observe, and reflect. I hear what is under the surface; how we are like one another.

I wrote this book the way that I did with the intent of having a conversation with you through printed words and your inner thoughts. If it helps, imagine us sitting on a couple of beach chairs, taking in the sunset as the waves crash onto the shore, just having a conversation about how to feed your needs and live the life you've dreamed of. It's closer than the horizon and you can have it if you choose.

In each chapter, I'll identify the problem and you'll see how it shows up in your daily life. You'll discover how to identify an unmet need, whether it's your own or someone else's. Next, I'll offer some solutions to meeting those needs, in you and in others.

Finally, each chapter will conclude with a self-assessment so you can figure out how you're doing on your path to having your needs met and living a life with less drama, fewer conflicts, and more joy. Use the book as a workbook, answering the questions and doing the exercises as you move through each section.

If you have a phobia about writing in books, *get over it*. I'm giving you permission to write in this one. Go ahead, scribble away. If that idea is too much for you, keep a notebook nearby and journal into it. Just please promise me that you will do the work and not just read the words. I want this book to work for you and you need to work at it for the best results. As I say to my kids and their friends, "we don't have problems here, only solutions. Let's figure this out, shall we?"

Buckle up, put your helmet on....this book can change your life. A little or a lot; it's all up to you. I hope you're reading this because you want change, because there is pain or discontent in your life that you want to stop. And you're hoping that this book holds the key to that. Fear not: It does. But you can't be passive: Not in life and not in using the tools and strategies in this book. You need to show up. Be accountable. Be consistent.

There are no quick fixes, but you can fix things quickly. Does it mean enough to you? Read on, dig deeply, and see yourself in the examples. Perform the exercises and do the end-of-chapter inventories. Go out and talk about what you've learned with friends and family.

Become the YOU that you were meant to be. Everyone else is already taken…

*"If you really want to be happy,
the only person that can stop you is you.
Don't strive to be happy. Be happy.
Wake up each morning. Smile. Look for the good in the day.
Choose to act happy. Find the good in others.
Work toward something larger than yourself.
Do the best you can in any endeavor." ~ Glenn Van Ekeren*

3

GROUND RULES

> "Life can only be understood backwards;
> but it must be lived forwards." ~Soren Kierkegaard

Before you get started on this book, we need to establish some ground rules, some filters. A few road signs that will help you navigate the terrain. These ground rules are really the basics of my world view. In fairness to you, I'm putting them right out there so that you can understand how I see the world and if it might be a fit for you. If it is, the rest of the book will feel like warm slippers, just the right size. Or, you might start off feeling like you're wearing a new pair of shoes and your toes are hurting. If you give it some time, you might stretch those babies out and fall in love with them. My hope is that you'll sense enough truth in these beliefs that you believe that the rest of this book will serve you well.

As I do in all of my coaching relationships, I put this information right up front. Love me or leave me, but know who you're dealing with before you take another step. The other reason I lay this out in the beginning is to set some realistic expectations about what this book can and cannot help you to do, and how you can use it to your fullest advantage. When I conduct workshops, I do the very same thing. If your expectations are different than what I can meet, we need to adjust those at the beginning so we can leave one another feeling heard, understood, and respected. Ready?

~Dysfunction Junction~

"It's not what happens to you
that determines how far you will go in life;
it is how you handle what happens to you." ~ Zig Ziglar

You've already read that you don't leave your problems and dysfunctions at home. You are every part of yourself all the time, whether you choose to showcase all of yourself or not. Either way, it's all up inside of you. So whether you're at home, school, or recreation activities, you bring YOU right in there. As I say in my workshops, you bring your "crazy" with you wherever you go.

The same goes for everyone else. No one leaves their crazy tucked safely in a locked closet where no one can see it. (Don't you wish they *could?*) And even though you might be more successful in feeding your needs with your family, for example, chances are that if you struggle in one place you do in other places, too.

Knowing this, I've written this book to address *your* struggles, confident that if you get your own "crazy" in order before you walk out your bedroom door, you'll be better equipped to handle other people's "crazy." Oh, and there is crazy. You know it's out there. Everywhere.

In addition to agreeing to that premise, the three things I need you to wrestle with before you hit the other chapters are what you *believe*, *choose*, and *release*. Each of these terms is defined so read on. I'll then offer an overview of how to use these practices to assist others in making the changes discussed in this book.

Do me (and yourself) a favor: Don't skip ahead. Trust me. If you don't read these sections first you'll end up in a tailspin of frustration. So, sit down. Settle in. Get comfortable. Soak it in. Reflect.

~Believe~

"We don't see things as they are,
we see them as we are." ~ Anais Nin

First, what you believe can help you to easily satisfy your needs. Belief is your orientation toward the world, toward information, toward other people, toward experiences. What do you believe about the world and your place in it? Do you believe in fate, or that you are in charge of your experiences, or a blend? Do you believe that the world is full of bad people who want to do you harm if you let your guard down? Or, do you believe that it's full of good people who may stumble sometimes, but they mean well? Does it change with circumstances or simply your mood? Here's your chance to journal about it.

<u>My belief system goes something like this:</u>
I think that the world:

I think that people:

I think that I:

Did you *actually* write anything down? If not, please <u>go back</u>. Before you go one page further in this book, I challenge you to examine what you believe and how you described it above. Read it to a friend or loved one and see if they agree. Is that the way that people see you?

Wrestle with that information a bit. See if you need to rewrite it. Ask your friends and loved ones again. Check it out and make sure you believe it. Own it if you believe it's working well for you. Vow to change it if it's not. There's no time like the present. And the fabulous thing about adolescence is that you're expected to change. Adults have a much tougher time. Just look at your parents and teachers. They are pretty stuck in their ways, aren't they? You? You can be one way today and another way tomorrow and the world will just chalk it up to hormones. That's a pretty convenient excuse, if you ask me. Milk that puppy for all it's worth!

Because here's the truth of the matter: You don't have endless tomorrows. You may be young, but you only live once. At least in this form and fashion. If the way you look at the world is hindering you and limiting your happiness and satisfaction, why not adjust it? Isn't it worth a shot? It's as simple as looking for information that confirms the more positive option. It's like the saying that pessimists are right more often, they're just less happy. Have you ever met someone who can take any situation and make themselves the victim in it, powerless to do anything? It's true that bad things happen and we are often on the receiving end of some pretty big headaches, but that doesn't mean that we have to filter everything through a victim lens. When we do, we attract more of the same.

> Plant rice, rice grows. Plant fear, fear grows.
> ~ Kung Fu

Have you read anything on the laws of attraction? If you haven't, please stop and Google it right now. According to the laws of attraction, what you *seek* is what you will *find*. If you expect mistreatment and sadness, you will find it, as sure as the sky is blue. Even if the person sitting in the seat right next to you went through the very same set of experiences, she might think it was a great gift while you're focused on it being a tragedy. The events didn't change.

Just the way you believe: Your worldview. The only thing that was different was how the very same experiences were interpreted.

It comes right down to whether you believe that the world is out to get you, or invested in your growth and joy. Even if something "bad" happens, if you have a positive view, you're likely to see it as bringing you a chance to learn something or grow from it somehow. If that doesn't sound inviting enough, just know that people with a more upbeat attitude suffer from fewer illnesses, have less stress, and live longer lives. Sold yet?

Not yet? In my master's program, I was drawn to a way of helping people called narrative therapy. The idea behind it is that the way you think and speak about things directly affects your feelings about them, and then how you act. Change the story, change your life. Have you ever met siblings who grew up in the same house yet think of their upbringings in very different ways? They hold onto certain images stronger than others. They select out what fits their filter about how life was.

But, wait! You mean that the same events can be responded to in wildly different ways? Yup. If when you think back on your life you feel victimized, abused, or mistreated, please do me a favor: Choose a new list of events to think about. If you need help in finding those events or shifting your thoughts, reach out for help. I was sent to therapists when I was young and I blew them off. Okay, I might have grabbed a few tidbits from all those hours in their office, but I was a pain in the ass. Seek out a trusted adult (preferably a real therapist) and ask for help on this. Tell them the real story, with all the ugliness. F it's really crappy, get help changing it, or simply surviving it, like I did. Then, if at all possible, ask for help making the shift away from that. Even the darkest of lives have some glitter in them. Start telling those sparkly stories to people you know. Feel the shift in your body. In your mind. In your spirit. It's a game changer. You can move through life with more energy, passion, positivity, and inspiring influence simply by telling your "story" differently.

Why does this happen? Because your mind and body react to the things you say. If you say depressing and frustrating things, you feel anger and sadness. If you say uplifting and positive things, you feel joy and peace. And it's not as hard as it sounds. It's like making a change in your diet: When you see a juicy bacon double cheeseburger you have to resist eating one every day if you don't want to die of a heart attack. When you find yourself telling sob stories about your existence, turn away from the grease-fest and pick up a yogurt parfait instead. Tell a happy anecdote. Recall a happy time. Live healthier and longer.

I spent countless years stuck in the rut of telling my "story" in a way that just served to hold me back in life. It's true that I had a great number of hellacious things happen in my life. It's just as true that I met my share of angels, laughed a ton, and celebrated abundance. After I took time with friends and therapists to acknowledge that I had been through hell, I was ready to let my perspective shift so that I didn't have to continue living in the "ick." When I started making the shift toward telling more of a balanced story (some good, some bad), my perspective shifted. My anxiety and depression lessened. I was able to tap into happy visions of my past, which led me to encouraging visions of my future.

This practice was enormously helpful as I moved through and past my divorce. I knew clearly why I left, and I had many stories to tell to explain. Juicy stories, full of all sorts of negative emotions. And I told my share of them to my friends. But I also told the funny ones. And there were lots of those. We had some good times. We shared some laughs. And I tell those to our children. If one comes to mind as we're doing something, I'd say, "oh, I remember one time when Daddy and I…" They love it. They are comforted, knowing that there were good times. And that I can embrace those. Unfortunately, their dad can't do the same. He's stuck with the other story. The story he continues to tell himself with only the negative experiences. And that can't feel good. And he is in charge of the stories he recalls and relives. And so are you.

I hope you're not caught up in your parents' divorce or conflict, but if you are, take a moment to reflect on the last paragraph. Sometimes people, including and especially adults, are stuck in a negative mindset. They haven't figured out how move on from bad experiences. They think they are right and they refuse to let go of their anger, probably for fear of what *not* being angry and resentful will feel like. Maybe they think if they're not angry someone will take advantage of them. They're stuck and, if they are your parent(s), you're affected by their decisions. Sorry, but it's the hard truth. And it sucks. I can put lipstick on that pig, but it's still a pig.

I know firsthand that this is not any fun. I can't tell you that they will change, because they might never change. Mine never did, not really. They got a little less toxic, but they died stuck. What I can tell you is that <u>you *can* change how you respond to them</u>. You have choices, too, and you can choose not hold smothering levels of anger toward them. Instead, you can see them as hurt and broken and stuck. If you do that, and resist the urge to let your anger and disappointment in them consume you, their sickness won't have control over you. You'll be free, even though you're living under the same roof. This level of detachment takes practice, but you can do it. You might need support, so reach out to a trusted adult to mentor you through it.

Sound weird or hard? Imagine you're watching a television show instead of being a part of it. Just watch them and see that their behavior is about them and where they are and not about you and where you are and can be. Let them act out their own story and focus on yours. That's what adolescence is all about: Creating your own identity and path, separate from your parents. If your parents are toxic or just moderately unhealthy, what better reasoning do you need to separate from their line of thinking and ways of behaving? Claim your own path and start living differently today. Let go of the anger now before it eats at you and comes out as anxiety, depression, eating disorders, or another dysfunction. I had a few instrumental adults in my life who helped me to recognize the craziness I was living in and I thank God for them. Do you have someone like that in your life? A teacher? Therapist? School counselor? One of your friend's parents? A relative? Pastor? As a mom (and former coach, religious education teacher, Girl Scout leader), I've been "that adult" to a number of kids (and still am). It's okay to ask for help and get another perspective on your problems. Adults have them, too, and if we're smart, we're asking for help. Just ask my therapist…

One warning: Loyalty is a valued trait in most families and if you start paving a healthy path when your family members are on a self-destructive one, they may see this as disloyalty. I know this happened in my family and it was a tough road to hoe. Tough, but well worth it. Wanna know more?

~Loyalty…And Family & Friends~

Being loyal is thought to be a crucial and positive trait in people. If you want to pay someone a compliment, call them loyal. People like to think of themselves as loyal because we take for granted that it's a good thing. Like any characteristic, it can be *good* or *bad*, depending on how and where it's applied. If it wasn't for a few key, trusted adults in my life when I was in middle school and high school I might be writing a very different book right now, from the comfort of my jail cell. I'm not being dramatic, I promise. Reach out to an adult you trust (teacher, coach, relative, friend's parent, therapist). Share your story. Ask for guidance. We're old. We know stuff.

Speaking of jail, in my volunteer work in the jail system in Virginia years ago, I conducted a class with inmates on family dynamics as it related to incarceration and criminal activity. One day, an inmate told a story about his father who used to tell him that he was useless and not worth a thing in this world, and that he'd amount to nothing. He spoke of his father with such disdain, speaking through his clenched jaw. After he finished his story, I asked him, "when are you going to stop being loyal to your father?"

I should pause here and describe myself physically so you can get a clear picture of what this moment looked like: I am a little bit of a thing. I couldn't drop kick a fly, let alone this 250 pound inmate who I'd just really ticked off.

He shot me a viscous look and said, "LOYAL? I'm not loyal to that man!" Undeterred, I repeated myself. By now a few other inmates started to nod and make noises that let me know that they were following my logic. After giving him time for another round of denial to the group, I said, "but, you've created the very life that he predicted for you. You've become his vision of you. You've made him right about you. That's the ultimate in loyalty: You gave up your own life to make him right."

Ouch. The weight of a dozen elephants, and a lifetime of suffering, looked like it rose right off of his shoulders as he pondered this. I believe his response was, "wow." Now I don't know what he did with this insight long-term, but hopefully he wrestled with it enough before he was released from jail and started making choices that served him and not his father's miserable vision of him. That's what I like to think anyway.

What about you? Can you be disloyal? And be proud of it? Teens are known for being rebellious. Can you be rebellious for the right reasons? I've chosen my happiness over loyalty more than once and I'm not going to sugar coat it: It's hard. When you make other people "wrong" about you and you refuse to be oppressed by their "crazy" they don't take too kindly to that. When you refuse to accept unhappiness even if it's the "safer" bet, people don't like to be left behind in their misery. You "belong" in that group/family: You need to stay, right?

Wrong. If you want to leave your baggage in the past (or hand it over to people who are trying to hijack your present) and embrace the idea of choice in your life, you get to choose what you will and won't tolerate in your life. You only get one life. Live it: In joy, from abundance, with love. For you first, and others next. That's not selfish, it's empowering. You can't feed others for long if you're starving to death. It doesn't work that way. Feed yourself first, and then feed others. More on this topic later in the book as we investigate how you pay attention first to your needs and then the needs of others.

~For Dating Teens~

Years ago, as I was getting back into the dating scene, I read a book that forever changed my life: "Fearless Loving" by Rhonda Britton. As a result of this book, I took ownership of my needs in a relationship. One of the exercises in her book instructed me to come up with a list of what I was looking for (my needs) and challenged me to never compromise on the "Top 5." They were deal breakers. Do not pass "go," do not collect $200, stop-right-there-features.

And I put them to the test. I not only carried them in my mind, but I discussed them openly. As I got into a relationship with someone and we started that "what are you looking for" conversation, I had my five and I made them known. I put them right out there. I won't tell you all five but here are two so you'll have a sense of what they look like: They seek to resolve (not start or avoid) conflict, and, they are passionate about me and about life in general. When it became clear after some time spent getting to know the other person and our "fit," I would have that "talk" and they always knew which one (or ones) of the five that were not "there" in the relationship.

Why was this important? I took full responsibility for my needs and didn't lapse back into a pattern of taking on their frustration or disappointment as my own or something I had to "fix." Since I'm still in contact with nearly every one of those men, I'm guessing that this approach wasn't a bad one. We faced why it wasn't working, and, why it wasn't going to work if there wasn't a shift. For me, it felt empowering to own my needs and not be apologetic for them. To know that it was okay to need what I needed and it didn't have to mean that either one of us was wrong if we didn't make a "love connection." It's just that we didn't *fit*. And that is okay. And I didn't feel guilty if they were hurt, sad, or angry when we broke up. I felt compassion, but I didn't let it suck me back into the relationship.

That book and those exercises taught me a very important life lesson: That I have my needs and my issues, and other people have their own. I have the responsibility for mine and I have no business getting into their drama. In a relationship, I can choose to try to feed their needs and help them with things in their life, but their happiness is not on my shoulders. And the reverse is true. And when I stay in that bubble and don't let the unhealthy and destructive patterns and demands of others to get into my head and my heart, I preserve myself for people who won't behave in that way. If I let them into my bubble, I risk being too exhausted and unhealthy to do anyone any good.

~Want Less Drama? Bubbles Rock!~

Are you ready to get in your own bubble? Your bubble is really cozy, and it's not lonely. As a matter of fact, your relationships will become more genuine and deeper because you won't be drawn into feeling guilty and responsible for problems that aren't yours. And you won't be burdening others with your baggage. Instead, you'll be seeing more clearly what belongs to you and what belongs to the other person so that you can relate to one another in a respectful and non-dramatic fashion.

Drama comes from people being outside of their bubble. I equate drama-based situations to the plant in "Little Shop of Horrors:" if you feed it, it just grows bigger and bigger. If you stay in your bubble when someone creates drama, you don't feed it. Unlike some of our other needs, drama-seeking behavior should not be rewarded with attention or it just breeds more of it. Resist the urge to add to it.

Instead, stay in your bubble, and observe the dramatic behavior. Try to figure out what need of the other person isn't being met and see if you can find a strategy to fill it in a less destructive and draining way.

I've found that the unmet need is usually *connection* and trying to feed that need with drama is highly ineffective, but a lot of people still rely on it. They won't own their real need, so they create a whole heap of drama to get attention. Instead of reacting aggressively toward the drama I suggest that you find another way to help the person feel connected to others that doesn't make you want to take a Xanax. Or go crazy on them. Neither of those options (acting aggressively or checking out completely), despite how much they may temporarily satisfy you, is recommended. Frankly, if you opt for either of those *you're* the one that'll end up facing negative consequences and that just doesn't help a thing, does it? What's the best option? Get in your bubble!

~Choose~

"Life isn't about finding yourself. Life is about creating yourself." ~George Bernard Shaw

When you saw this book you may have thought to yourself, "Oh, I know some people who drive me nuts. It looks like this book will be the magic carpet I need to get them to change." Or, maybe your inner voice sounded something like this, "Ugh. I want to be happier. And, as soon as I figure out how, all the people around me need to step up and do the same." Trust me: I would love to promise the magic carpet you want, but "Genie" is not in my name. As for wanting other people to follow in your footsteps, that would be awesome. The truth of the matter is that they may not change one bit, but if *you* do, *you* will be happier, healthier, more productive, and more successful. Sound good?

Can these lessons change your personal relationships? They can, but only *your* part of it. No one gets to decide how *you* live except for *you*. You choose. So, you don't get to decide how someone else is going to live. Sure, you can complain about how stupid, crazy, wasteful, idiotic, destructive, etc. the behaviors of others are, but those behaviors are theirs to display. They get to decide what they want, just like you get to decide what you want. They choose for them. You choose for you. The more time and energy you spend trying to change the behaviors of others is less time you get to spend enjoying the blessings that you have in your own life. This includes your parents, siblings, friends, family members, and boyfriends/girlfriends. And all the people you have conflict with. They are the drivers in their own lives and they own their own crazy. And you own yours.

Now, I know it's tempting to "help," but as my father (a self-destructive force to be reckoned with) said, "you can't help a person who isn't willing to accept your help." And, boy, was he right. If I'd listened to him, really heard what he was saying when he said it, I'd have saved myself a ridiculous amount of pain and suffering. I was fifteen, and although I knew he was talking about himself, I still held onto the thought that I was Wonder Woman and I could make things different with and for him if I just tried harder. I thought I had the bracelets and the tiara and everything. In truth, I was holding out for a miracle and feeling super responsible for its absence.

If you see yourself in that story, please don't live like that for one more minute. Not one more. Please. It's such a waste of breath and energy and love. You can *want* things for others. That's a beautiful thing to do. You can pray for them. You can share your insights and experiences with them. But at the end of the day, and at the beginning of each new one, they get to decide how they want to live. And some people prefer misery, they really do.

You know these people: They are offered chance after chance to be in a better life and they keep choosing to be in sorrow, in defeat, in anger, at war. That's their "happy." It's where they are most comfortable. And, only if they have an epiphany or their soul gets tired of being so weighed down will they seek long-term relief. If not, they are committed to staying there in that heavy, ugly space. They are choosing to be right about life and how horrible it can be over being happy with it. Bullies are a lot like this, no matter how "happy" they many seem on the outside. Bullies are the most insecure, sad, and angry people out there. Don't let their fake smiles fool you. They are miserable on the inside.

Being right over being happy. Imagine that? Have you ever made that choice? I know I have. In an argument, for sure. I've found myself so committed to proving my point that I lose sight of my larger goal: To be happy and loved. So, it's not such a foreign concept that there are people who choose to be right over being happy all the time. They believe that the world is a bad place. They behave accordingly. And guess what? It's bad. If they were open to thinking good things about the world, they would be proven wrong about the world being a crappy place. So they choose being "right." You'll read more on this in the "release" section of this chapter because it's worthy of deep discussion. I wonder how tight your grip is? But, I digress. Let's get back to our talk about choice.

Choice is the number one thing in a healthy, positive, and productive life. Years ago, I spoke to my daughter's elementary school class about volunteer work that I had done as they were doing a segment on community service. The volunteer work I'd done was with inmates at a county jail, both male and female. One of the kids asked how the inmates ended up in "there." How I responded was so simple that this second grader could understand it, yet many adults still can't grasp it. I said that sometimes people make a series of bad choices and at some point on that path, they break a law or laws and have to go to jail as a punishment. Other times, they just make one really bad choice to end up there.

It comes right down to choices. It's really that simple. Good decision or bad decision. It's all your choice. Even when you think that you have "no choice," you always have two options, at a minimum. You don't believe me? Test me. It's true. You always have a choice. Always. I will grant you that sometimes those options don't seem like real options. But they are options. To act is always the clearest option. But inaction is also a choice. If there is a gun to your head, you still have a choice. It's not a good one, for sure, but it's a choice. You think your parents or teachers or coaches are in charge of you and your life?

You're wrong. They may control a great deal of things, but you get to choose how you respond to them and how you feel and think about your circumstances. That's a lot of control. A LOT.

When you're faced with a situation, you can choose to respond (in a host of ways), wait to respond, or decide that no response is best. And you always get to choose *how* to respond, whether it's with anger and resentment, sorrow and hopelessness, or joy and hopefulness. That is your choice. No one chooses that for you. They may make it hard on you. They may darken the room and make it harder to find the door. They *influence* you. But you can feel your way through that space and *choose*.

Do you need an example to see if this "choose" thing fits for you? I call this little story "moldy meatloaf." Grossed out? Don't worry: It's not really about moldy meatloaf. But hold onto your nausea because it will help illustrate the moral of the story.

Example: Moldy Meatloaf. I was speaking with a coaching client of mine who was complaining about his "inability to finish reading a book." As we discussed this, it came out that he has finished plenty of books in his lifetime. Sometimes it only takes him two or three days to blast through a book. So his statement was factually wrong. He isn't unable to finish a book. I wondered if the difference was the type of book? Nope. He'd read nonfiction and fiction books cover-to-cover as much as he'd stopped reading them mid-stream.

After pointing out the lie he was telling himself (that he doesn't finish books when he clearly has finished a large pile of them), I asked him why he tends to stop a book in the middle. He described a few reasons: Subject matter was boring, repetitive, or just didn't hold his interest. Okay, now we were getting somewhere.

Instead of congratulating himself for not wasting more of his precious time on lousy reads and criticizing the unskilled authors, he owned it as his "failure."

I threw out a hypothetical case to him: Pretend he and I were good friends. We were honest with one another and never faked a thing.

One night he comes to my house for dinner and I serve him meatloaf. He's heard all about my famous meatloaf and is excited to try it.

At first he's enjoying it. He gets about midway through the slice and notices that there is mold all over the remaining half. Ewwwww. What would he do? Would he smile pretty and eat it? He laughed and said that he'd tell me he wasn't going to eat another bite. I was relieved, since as his coach, I would have had a tough time if he'd said that he'd eat it. Barf.

So, why did he feel he had to finish a book that was bad? I thought maybe it was the wasted money, but he gets his books from the library so he doesn't pay a cent. What was it then? We concluded that when he chose to "quit" he thought that made him a "quitter." That somehow, if he chose to start something he had to choose to not only continue it but also to finish it. You might be thinking, "yeah, of course. You're supposed to finish what you start." Okay, fair enough. That sounds great on paper. But what if it's moldy meatloaf? Are you ready to finish that? Slather on some ketchup and fake it, hoping you don't wretch it up later?

I'm not proposing that you walk away from things when they pose a challenge. You've got to stick with things, as a general rule. I'm simply pointing out the fact that every word, thought, behavior, and action is a choice. Starting something. Finishing something. Walking away from something. You get to choose. You can choose to let the world choose for you. That's a choice, too. And there are consequences to every choice (moldy meatloaf on your breath, for one), whether you make that choice consciously or not. Why would you choose to waste your time reading a book you don't like? Would you rather choose intentionally for yourself and deal with the consequences, or sit back and be a passenger in your own life? The choice is, and always has been, yours.

So what will you do the next time you start something and later find yourself in the middle of it, without any motivation to do anything more? Will you ask yourself "why?" and wait for the answer? To see if it's something you fell into and really don't have any interest in seeing to completion? Or decide that you want to get it done, using a reward on the other end of it so that you reach the finish line? Please just remember one thing: It makes no sense to wallow in regret, shame, and guilt if finishing it really isn't going to make you a better person or the world a better place. Your energies can be used better elsewhere. Recognize the choices available to you. Choose wisely. If not, get the ketchup ready. (Ewwwwww!)

~Release~

"It's not the load that breaks you down, it's the way you carry it."
~Lou Holtz

Like DNA and fingerprints, we all have unique things that weigh us down as we make our way through the world. Bad experiences, hurt feelings, disappointments, and frustrations that left their mark on us. You might be a light traveler, with all your baggage fitting in a backpack you sling easily over your shoulder. You might be an average traveler, with a carry-on and a rolling suitcase. Or, you might be unable to travel because, like a guest star of "Hoarders," you're so weighed down in "stuff" you can't even get out from under it, let alone travel.

Which traveler are you? How much baggage do you have? Are you weighed down by emotions and hurts from the past? How much are you blaming past events and players in your life for the troubles and struggles you face? When something "bad" happens, is your response something like, "well, that figures. It's just like when so-and-so did such-and-such. This always happens. If it weren't for so-and-so and such-and-such, my life would have been and would be so much better." Sound familiar? If so, you've got some unpacking to do. You're playing the blame game and you're going to end up the loser. Do you resent other people having control over your life? Then stop letting their past behavior have control over your present state of mind. If they are still acting badly and you're stuck being in contact with you, you can still release their hold over you. No one gets to choose your thoughts or your feelings for you. You're in charge. So, get in charge.

In order to unpack the past, you have to be willing to release those events and hurts that are holding you back from taking each new moment as a new moment and reliving all the bad stuff that's happened to you. You need to loosen your grip on those things that hold you back. And, tougher still, you need to let go. Ready?

There are a few key elements in the release process. They all are critical to releasing yourself from the burdens of things that have happened. There is no magic wand. It's going to take work. Please be aware that the last one is the hardest for most people, so I need to stretch your muscles before we get to the "f" word. They key elements are: *Push*, *Prosper*, and *Forgive* (ooooh).

~Push~

"Nobody can hurt me without my permission."
~ Mahatma Gandhi
"*...Don't give them permission.*"
~ Jessi Cooper

One of the biggest issues I encounter with people is the challenge in figuring out what their baggage is and what belongs to someone else. When you have *boundary issues* it's a huge challenge to figure out what is your baggage and what belongs to someone else. You either blame others for all of the problems in your life or you take on everybody's troubles and actions as if they were your own and your fault. You don't know your *boundaries*.

You want more happiness and less stress? It comes down to the simplest task: Creating boundaries. Letting other people own their "stuff" while you own yours.

When you have firm boundaries you can sit back and observe as others run around you in a state of utter craziness. Imagine the power. You don't feel the crazy. You don't try to fix the crazy. You may try to open the window to let some crazy out, or maybe comment on the crazy to make sure that you've done your part to demonstrate your awareness of it.

You *can* resist taking on drama that does not belong to you. You *can* resist trying to fix others or their situation. You recognize that they must be meeting some need to continue with this ridiculous behavior. But you feed your needs in other ways, so you can just *watch* without entering the fray.

Have you seen someone with a strong sense of themselves and they don't get caught up in other people's drama? Someone who stands there and just observes without participating? Who can sit in the caf or walk down the halls and not get triggered by the voices and faces all around him/her?

I've mentored teens who have managed to do just that and they are so much happier. They've recognized that hurt people hurt people. Say that out loud.

Hurt people hurt people.

So, if there is someone out there who is hurting you on purpose, quickly realize that they are in pain. Sound like a bully you know? They may seem quite confident but I assure you that they are hurting inside because people who aren't in pain don't try to bring pain to others.

If you think about when you're been hurtful toward other people it's always when you were in pain yourself. You lashed out because you were in a bad space. The person on the receiving end might have triggered some of your anger, but if you did something hurtful (with the intent of hurting the other person), that said something about *you*, not *them*.

Before I got the hang of boundaries, I thought people who stayed "detached" and out of the drama must be drugged, stupid, or numbed out to the world. Now I am the one considered suspect.

~*Magic Bubbles*~

At one holiday function a few years ago, my sister asked me what I was "on" because I was so calm. She couldn't understand that I was "high" on boundaries. I was in what I have affectionately come to call my "B-Bubble" (pronounced "Buh Bubble" for those audio book lovers out there). Like being in an impenetrable bubble, when I'm in my B-Bubble, the crazy, anxiety-provoking, maddening behavior that others display just bounces right off the surface and isn't allowed into my mental space. I'm a very visual person, so sometimes I revel in imagining their craziness ricocheting off the Plexiglas, and splashing back onto them. "Ha, ha! You've got your crazy back!"

Sound fun? Want to use this tactic? Change the first letter of B-Bubble to the first letter of your name (If your name is Joe, it's your "J-Bubble"). Imagine their shock when what they thought was going to burst your bubble flies right back at them? It's strangely satisfying to experience other people having to hold their own anxiety and negative behaviors and not able to take them out on you. And it's surprisingly soothing for those around you; I have learned this for myself.

Awhile back, I was at a dress rehearsal for my daughters' dance recital. One of the other moms, was losing her mind. The perfectionist dance instructor was making people crazy with her demands and this woman was pacing back and forth trying to keep up with what she needed to do next to please the lady. She approached me to complain and she was *floored* by my calm. I shared my B-Bubble concept with her.. She loved it, of course, because she was exhausted and holding my own boundaries calmed her. I didn't add to her anxiety by letting her feelings affect my own. I didn't build her worry tower taller. I didn't offer any bricks for the tower, just calm.

Now, before you go thinking that I come from a long line of Buddhists, let me set the story straight. I won't go into the details of my early years, but suffice it to say that I thought everything and everyone existed in some emotionally life-sucking dependence. Where others ended and I began was a foreign concept to me — as incomprehensible as walking upside down on the ceiling. I was a poster child for co-dependence for a long, long, LONG time. I thought everything was my fault and my responsibility. It was oppressive and cost me a great deal in lost time and squandered happiness.

So I now get a great deal of satisfaction from being able to resist jumping in and trying to fix everything. I say, "Oh" a lot. As in, "Oh, you seem upset." Or, "Oh, you look mad about that." And, "Oh, you seem bothered by what's going on."

What did I used to say? Things like: "I'm sorry, I didn't mean to do that." Or, "I'm sorry, what can I do to fix that?" And, "You poor thing, what can I give you to make you feel better?" Do you recognize yourself in this? Do you find yourself saying "I'm sorry" a lot?

On the surface, these may seem like caring and polite things to say. And they are. But only if you're *not* taking on the responsibility for making others feel better. That's on *them*. That is their job to own. You own your contribution, they own the final result.

Regardless of your age, healthy relationships are like that: You own your stuff and I own mine. And we talk about the acreage in the middle of us: The relationship that joins us together. I don't try to squish myself into your bubble or suck you into mine. We are individuals, with unique experiences and feelings and thoughts. You're not responsible for mine and I'm not responsible for yours. And you can be upset, and I don't have to fix it. I don't have to assume responsibility for your hurt or anger; however, I can (and must) if it's partly mine. Under <u>no</u> circumstances do I claim responsibility in order to make you feel better. That does you absolutely no favors.

~*Prosper* ~

"Whether you think you can, or you think you can't:
you're right." ~Henry Ford

In order to leave the past in the past and to take on new moments as new moments, you have to come from a place of wanting to prosper and live in joy and gratitude. At its core, this means preferring to be <u>happy</u> over being <u>right</u>. Who would prefer to be right over being happy? Plenty of people. Why would someone *do* that?

One of the easiest illustrations of this is the tendency to hold onto a low, limiting opinion of your own worth and potential. Maybe someone (or some series of people) have told you at some point along the way that you aren't good enough somehow. That you are flawed in some pivotal way that predicted that you won't amount to much. You aren't pretty enough. Smart enough. Thin enough. Capable enough. Coordinated enough. Confident enough. Funny enough. Talented enough. You aren't *enough*. And some space in your psyche believes those messages and you've taken them on as truth. You've not only listened to them, but you've begun to live out those messages. You are operating under these messages and you're looking for evidence to prove them right. How do you do that? You fail, fall short, and experience (self-imposed) limitations. You live <u>their</u> truth about you.

What if that isn't the truth about *you*, but instead it is the truth about *them*? We tend to see others in a way that serves us. We push people lower if we feel low so that *we* don't feel as low. It's a sad aspect of human nature. People who feel on top of the world typically try to raise other people higher, to share the view from the top. There is plenty of sunshine to go around up here. People at the bottom of the heap tend to need to step on others to see daylight.

There is no time like the present to adopt a mindset to prosper. Can you give up the pull to prove those negative voices right about you? Can you form new opinions of new possibilities about you? Can you see that you are limited only by your vision of yourself? There is a huge statement tucked in there, so return to it for a second. You are limited only by your vision of yourself. What IS your vision of yourself? Is it a limiting one, or an ever-expanding one? Are you resting in the safety of being right about that damaged "you" that you perceive? Do you feel it's easier to fail (or worse yet, not even try) then to expect success?

Here's the truth: You might not succeed. If you expect success, you *might* be wrong. Horror! But, what if you're right? What if you succeed? If you fall short of perfection, of course, but you reap abundance? Would that bring more happiness to your life? You bet it would. As you learned (or will learn) in physics class, for every action there is an equal reaction. If you stop believing those voices from the past (or maybe they are still present in your world?), you will commit a sin against these naysayers: You will be disloyal. Remember our discussion on loyalty? It's your choice. Make the right one.

~*Forgive*~

"Forgiveness is letting go of all hope for a better past."
~ Unknown

I said it. Well, I typed it. The "f" word. Not *that* "f" word. The harder one to say: Forgive. Of all of the concepts that people seem to struggle with the most it's forgiveness, hands down. Why is that? It was one of the biggest stumbling blocks in my path, personally. Maybe like you I had some pretty terrible things done to me as a kid, yet I was instructed to forgive those who committed those acts. It was the "good girl/daughter" thing to do. And I was made to feel guilty and told that there was something wrong with me because I wouldn't forgive those who had hurt me. I had such a hard time with this from so many angles. I thought of myself as a kind, giving, loving person, so why couldn't I forgive?

I watched shows on it. Read books on it. Discussed it with friends and therapists. I got no closer to an answer no matter what I tried. I was stuck. And I was holding onto a whole boatload of anger and resentment. And it was eating me from the inside out.

Shortly after my divorce, I read a book that forever changed my life. The book, "The Shack," was passed along to me at a book club I joined when I moved to a new town. It's a tough read for a parent as the storyline is about a father who has a crisis of faith after his young daughter is murdered. In the book, he comes face to face with God and twists himself into an emotional pretzel when God challenges him to forgive the murderer. Imagine that? Forgiving the person who murdered your daughter? Unthinkable. But then God explains that there are two pieces to forgiveness: Letting go of the emotional attachment (rage, anger, resentment, thoughts of retaliation) to the offender, and deciding how or if you want to be in a relationship.

"Wait a hot second!" I thought to myself. "I can let go of the anger, etc. and still decide that the person doesn't get to be in relationship with me?" Or, I get to not trust them because they are likely to behave the same way again, but I can still let go of the anger and resentment? Yup. I sure could. And I did that quite a few times after that. As the author presented, you might decide that the person is apt to hurt you again because they are unhealthy. So, you can limit or even end your relationship with them in order to protect yourself from future injury. And, at the same time, you can let go of the "ick factor" of emotions that tied you to that person. Because if you think about it, do you really want to be attached emotionally to a person with all that ick? Or maybe attached to them at *all*?

I challenge you to write a list of the people in your life that you haven't forgiven. Who are you holding a grudge against? Next to their names, write a note about what they did. Now pause. Have they done that same thing over and over again, without truly apologizing and changing their behavior? Are they likely to continue to behave that way in the future? If so, does it make sense to limit your relationship with them? Or is it so toxic and unhealthy that it needs to be ended? This all comes down to an issue of trust:

Trust people to be *who* they are and *where* they are and you won't be disappointed.

If they are in an unhealthy place, trust *that* and act accordingly. Don't trust a dog to watch your sandwich. Think about that for minute. It seems stupid to trust a dog to watch your sandwich, right? So, why would you trust someone who is untrustworthy? If you do, *you* are really the one most at fault. You can't blame the dog for doing what is in his nature and what you knew he was inclined to do. He's a *dog*. And, yes, people are a lot like dogs: They are true to character. So trust *that* and you won't be disappointed. And you won't waste your valuable time trying to make a dog trustworthy enough to be left alone with your lunch. I'll leave you with one more quote about forgiveness to help you along.

"Forgiveness is not the misguided act of condoning irresponsible, hurtful behavior. Nor is it a superficial turning of the other cheek that leaves us feeling victimized and martyred. Rather it is the finishing of old business that allows us to experience the present, free of contamination from the past." ~ Joan Borysenko

~Backpack Theory~

Now that you've wrestled with these basics, read on. As you do, keep in mind that the more that you're aware of what goes on inside of you and around you, the more options you'll have for responding. And, the more that you practice your options, the more skilled you'll become at choosing the best option in any given scenario. It reminds me a lot of "Minecraft" (my daughters are hooked on it). I'm old school, so I call this my "backpack theory." When you try new things, you add a behavior option to your "backpack." You're not locked into a knee-jerk reaction. You have choices in how you respond. You build confidence in your abilities to do a variety of things in any situation.

It's a lot like cooking: If you only know how to boil pasta, when you get hungry, you make pasta. On the other hand, if you learn how to fry chicken, broil steak, and grill burgers, you have so many more choices when you're hungry. As you read this book, I highly recommend that you do the exercises, talk with friends and family about what you're learning, and try applying the lessons in your everyday life. Your backpack will be bursting at the seams in no time at all. And having choices makes you an abundantly more healthy, happy, and productive person. What have you got to lose? Just the pleasure a good life offers…

~Bottom Line~

Spend some time establishing a relationship with *yourself*. Don't be afraid to be alone, by choice or not. The best way to be a good friend/companion to others is to be one to yourself. Hating on yourself isn't attractive. Putting yourself down constantly isn't healthy or fun to be around. It puts a lot of pressure on the people around you to convince you to think otherwise. If you feel badly about yourself, it's time to do some work on yourself. Work to change what you don't like or work to get over it. It's annoying to listen to someone complain about something that they "hate" about themselves…and witness them doing nothing to change it. Step up or shut up.

Too harsh? Too bad. If you want your life to be better it does you zero good for me to sugar coat it. If you *do* look fat in those jeans do you really want me to tell you that you don't? If your hair looks like crap do you really want me to tell you it looks fabulous? Really? No. Fix your hair before you bump into your crush looking like the Heat Miser. Please. I know we don't know each other but I'd like to rise to "friend" status and I'm not earning your trust if I'm not honest and firm with you. You're young, but the length of your time on this planet isn't guaranteed so stop wasting your time being mad, sullen, meek, and self-abusing. Ain't nobody got time for that. I know this first hand, I swear.

If I could reclaim any period of my life it'd be my teens. I was angry, depressed, and I beat myself up like a pro boxer. I was awful to myself. And I thought I had good reasons. And I carried that nonsense into my 20s which produced some pretty toxic romances. Fun is! Knock that junk off, please. Your life, and all the positive energy you can send out, is an amazing blessing no matter how much ick you have going on. Your job is to figure out how to share your gifts, your essence, with the world. In all its glory. No excuses. You don't have to have all of the answers. You can't, it's not possible. Just take the next right step. Yes, that means keep reading this book.

"All endings are also beginnings.
We just don't know it at the time." ~ Mitch Albom

Ground Rules

~End of Chapter Inventory~

"The difference between ordinary and extraordinary
is that little extra." -- Jimmy Johnson

Summary: This chapter provided a framework from which all of the concepts in this book emerge. In order for you to understand how to address your needs and the needs of others you must know the author's worldview and assumptions.

Key Concepts:
- There are three actions that you can take to change your life: Believe, Choose, and Release.
- In order to Release, you must Push, Prosper, and Forgive.
- The Backpack Theory encourages you to take a risk and try something new as much as possible in order to increase your response options.

What are three takeaways you have from this chapter? What did you learn about yourself and/or others? What shifts in thinking did you experience as a result of reading this chapter?

Takeaway 1:

Takeaway 2:

Takeaway 3:

Rate yourself on your confidence and competence practicing the key concepts in this chapter:

1: I'm so lousy I don't want to respond

2

3

4

5: I'm okay, but I have a lot to learn

6

7

8

9

10: I'm going to write my own book on this competency

What are three things you commit to do (differently) as a result of reading this chapter? Think of things that will improve your life personally, spiritually, emotionally, and physically.

Commitment 1:

Commitment 2:

Commitment 3:

What are three roadblocks/challenges to being where you need to be? In other words, what are three things (relationships, habits, assumptions, situations) that you need to adjust and/or remove in order to live happier?

Roadblock 1:

Roadblock 2:

Roadblock 3:

What are three strategies for addressing those roadblocks and challenges? What are three changes you could make that would reduce or remove the obstacles you have?

Strategy 1:

Strategy 2:

Strategy 3:

"And, when you want something, all the universe conspires in helping you to achieve it." ~ Paulo Coelho

4

CONNECTION & PRESENCE

"Some people feel the rain.
Others just get wet." ~Bob Marley

As human beings, we are all pretty complex. Yet, we hold some essential elements in common. We all have needs. Aside from the basic needs of food, water, and shelter, we have a whole host of personal and interpersonal needs. One of the core needs is the need for connection. We are social creatures and have a basic drive to be with other people, to be seen and understood, and to be known and loved. Not just *told* that you're loved. But *feel* that you're loved. Feeling like you're important to someone. Feeling like you matter a great deal to someone who cares about you and what you value. That someone "gets" you.

Did you ever have a friend or family member who you could go weeks or months without talking to and as soon as you got on the phone or met up, it was like no time had passed at all? You had a rhythm. You could finish each other's thoughts. You knew what would make them smile, so you did it, and they did the same for you. When they listened to you, they really listened. They heard you. And you did the same for them. That's *connection*.

As you pass through life and experience heartbreaks, the pain comes from <u>having</u> and then <u>losing</u> a connection. Or, it comes from the pain of never having that connection at all. Imagine a life without those needs being met? Sad as it may seem, some of us go through our whole lifetime without feeling that connection except for fleeting moments here and there. Have you been lucky enough to feel it yet?

We need to be connected to other people: It's our human essence. Some of us get that we need to connect at a deep level. Or, we might go through life and only connect with others at the surface. That saying, "too close for comfort" applies here: You might find that there is only so much connection you're comfortable with. And that's what you seek. Comfortable. Safe. And you surround yourself with others who want that same depth of closeness. You're okay with being "buddies" but not friends. Oh, you might bump into someone who wants more than you want, but that causes all sorts of discomfort, so like music that's too loud, you turn it down or turn it right off. What's your "connection volume?" How close do *you* want to be to other people?

"Wake me up when it's all over. When I'm wiser and I'm older.
All this time I was finding myself and
I didn't know that I was lost." ~ Avicii

~Connection is Connected~

That's pretty deep, huh? Connection is connected. Wow. I'm pretty smart, aren't I, coming up with that all on my own? I suppose I could just leave it there and hope you get the message. Truth be told, I just wanted to make sure you were still "with" me and not lost in some episode of your favorite television episode or some vine. With me?

The thing about connection is that it is such a core human need that it has tentacles that reach out to every other core need discussed in this book. That's why I put it right up front: I wanted you to master the material on this one need before you tackle the rest. Because the rest of the needs are intertwined (I resisted the urge to say "connected!") with this one. Connection is tied to Control.

45

Connection and Validation have a great deal in common. And, Connection goes hand in hand with Passion and Purpose. You don't believe me? Let's address them briefly one by one.

Passion and purpose hinge on feeling connected to something or someone. As human beings, we need to know that we matter. If there is no connection, there is no passion, no feeling of purpose. With deep connection anything seems possible, and this is at the core of passion.

Control, and its balance or imbalance in our lives, speaks to our connection to ourselves, others, and our higher power (like God or Buddha or Allah or a non-descript entity like the Universe). Sometimes our efforts at control exist to keep us bonded to other people or things. When we feel a balance of control in our lives (on the spectrum between letting go and holding on), we feel less stress and more comfort in the world and people around us.

Validation rests squarely on the shoulders of connection. If you are feeling connected in a positive way to someone, you show recognition and appreciation freely. When you are shown authentic validation and get the sense that someone approves of you, you feel more connected.

To be honest, I could have written an entire book just on the need for connection and looked at every other need through that lens. Our connections are at the center of our needs: Feeling a passion and purpose in them, understanding the role of control and influence in them, and the validation of them. As you digest and apply the ideas in this book, just know that if you understand and embrace the importance of connection, the rest will come a whole lot easier.

~Me First!~

Maybe it's because I'm the "baby" sister, but I'm putting "me first" right up front in this whole connection discussion. Here's the cold, hard truth: If you're not connected to YOU, you're not really connected to anyone else. You're just a shell to other people. That old adage, "love yourself first before you try to love anyone else" is a complete truism. You must. And to truly love yourself you must be connected to yourself.

How do you get connected to you? You need to pay yourself some attention. You need to listen to the cues your body gives to you. How are you feeling right now? Really feeling? What is your body telling you? Do you have tension? Nervousness? Anxiety? Anger? Excitement? Joy? When was the last time that you paid attention to your toes? Yes, your toes. Not just when they were squished in tight shoes or you stubbed them on a doorway. When you were just sitting down. Like right now. Go ahead and take a minute to wiggle them. Feel how they connect to your foot, and your ankle. Are they tense or relaxed? How about your lips? Pucker them, lick them, feel them. As you breathe, can you feel your chest rise and fall. Is it tight or relaxed? Does it feel odd to be this in touch with your body?

Most people go through life not even knowing what's going on in their bodies unless they feel intense pain or pleasure. Are we that busy to not even know our own bodies? You bet. We are on auto-pilot most of the time and fail to take the time to attend to our physical selves in a real way. And sometimes it has to do with what we have done or have *had done* to our bodies. For survivors of physical or sexual abuse, we left our bodies to escape the trauma. And some of us never fully returned.

Thirty-some-odd years after my body was first abused, I was in a relationship where, for the very first time in my life, I was conscious of every cell in my body when we touched. It was bizarre. I had no idea I had all those nerve endings. It was beautiful yet somewhat disturbing because that experience stood in sharp contrast to the numbness I had experienced all of my life to that point. It struck me that I probably wasn't alone in going through life only half alive. I was not really in touch with my whole self with any sort of regularity.

This was an awakening. And I committed to myself that I would work hard on my connection to myself, not just in an emotional way, but a physical one. Are you ready to do the same? Can you make it a daily practice to sit with yourself for even a minute or two and just feel what is going on inside of your body? I have zero proof to back me up here, but I have a strong feeling that doing that will allow you to feel when something isn't quite right with your body, long before a sharp pain sets in or a bad test result comes back. And that is a very, very good thing.

~Focus~

"At some point, I finally realized that stress made a really bad companion...so I had it pack its shit and leave." ~ Steve Maraboli

Focus, the limited amount (or complete lack) of it, is the number one complaint that clients approach me with as they enter coaching. Usually, though, they don't use that specific word. Instead, they talk to me about being "overwhelmed" and "stressed out." About not having enough time in the day to get the things done that need to get done. About being pulled in a hundred directions and juggling multiple balls all day long. They want more *time*.

Their sleep patterns are interrupted. Often their tempers are short. Many have weight issues because they use food for something other than nutrition, and they stuff their faces with unhealthy snacks as they run from activity to activity. Some use alcohol or other drugs to calm their nerves. Their health is often affected, with their bodies echoing what their minds are saying: "stop this train, I want to get off!" Who could blame them? There is little satisfaction in that existence.

Does this sound at all like you? Are you ready to stop that pattern? Keep reading and start the process of making your life significantly better.

First, we need to define "connection" so we can see what "focus" has to do with "connection." In our personal relationships, connection means some level of love or caring mixed with a sense of being known and understood. I used to say that one of my purposes in life was to *love*. As beautiful a purpose as that was, it missed the mark for me. I can love people all day and all night and still not feel satisfied. What if they don't love me back? What if they don't treat me well? What if I feel invisible around them? What if they love me for how I serve them but not for who I am? That's love, yet it's hollow and dissatisfying.

What's missing? Connection. Feeling like you and the other person are on the same page. Like you are being paid attention to and you mean something. It's when you feel like someone is holding your hand even when they are not even there. It's the opposite of having a conversation with someone who is consumed by their phone or tablet: They aren't paying real attention to you. When you don't have that connection and focus, you could be sitting right next to someone and feel lonely, like you're the only person in the world. It's such a tragic feeling.

The late Robin Williams said it best, "I used to think that the worst thing in life was to end up alone. It's not. The worst thing in life is to end up with people who make you feel all alone." So many of us have found ourselves in relationships where this is the case. You'd prefer to actually be alone rather than be with that person and feel shut out.

Maybe you have friends who just take up space in your life but aren't really seeing you for who you really are. If you're dating, maybe you're in a dead-end romance. Perhaps you're drifting through life without slowing down to truly be in the moment with friends and/or loved ones?

The time to change that is now. Tolerating a numb life now is just setting you up to continue that pattern into adulthood. And the older you get, the harder it is to change your habits. Trust me. Old dogs and new tricks and all that jazz. This is an invitation to feel some compassion for your parents and all of their missteps. They might also be drifting through life, unaware or feeling unable to change anything. They are stuck and they don't know how to move forward to a different existence. And that affects you, I'm sure. How many times have you said to your parents, "you don't understand! You're not even listening to me!" I'm not letting them off the hook for causing you pain as they walk their path; I'm only suggesting that you find some inspiration in their choices to make different ones for yourself. *Functioning* and *living* are two different things. As with everything in life, it's your choice. Make the best one. And consider taking the lessons you're learning in this book to try to connect better with other people; to give them your focus, your undivided attention.

~Build Connection...Through Presence~

"Live a little, love a lot." ~ Kenny Chesney

When I had just finished my first year of college, I was home on break visiting friends and found myself at the house of a former boyfriend. We were sitting alone in his kitchen, just talking. I was sitting on his counter and he was facing me and he was giving me grief because I wouldn't look him in the eyes. I would, but for a fleeting second, and then I would look down or away. He challenged me to look at him, to have some sort of a staring contest. I was embarrassed because I couldn't seem to manage to look into his eyes for more than a couple of seconds at a time.

We played this game for a while, until I got so uncomfortable that I jumped down from the counter and left his house shortly thereafter. That moment sticks in my mind, even though it was over 25 years ago, because it revealed to me that my ability to truly connect with another person, to be vulnerable to them and be authentically present with them, was severely stunted. Why? What was I so afraid of? It wasn't physical: My eyes weren't broken. It was something inside of me. I resisted being connected and fully present with others.

Over the years, I worked at this "eye contact challenge" and this idea of "presence" with varying degrees of success. But my awareness of it was forever changed by that moment in his kitchen. Now, in my work with clients, one of the core skills that I work with them on is *presence*. Being in union with the *moment* and the *person* you are with, not distracted by the past or the future. It's amazing what eye contact can do! Holding that calm, clear, caring state of being is not easy. And it is made more difficult when there is not abundant trust in the other person.

Through much trial and error, I've learned that you can be present to another person even if they are angry, hurt, untrustworthy, or lacking any ability to be present themselves. To be honest, I've experienced a phenomenal level of peace when I am in that state of intentional presence with a person who is hateful, raging, and even threatening. I've come to believe that this is so because I am not feeding the negative energy and I am able to speak and act with thought and not tangled emotion. I'm distant on a personal level, not allowing their "ick" to destroy my mental health. Yet, I'm present to them, feeling compassion for them. I'm not injured by their hate or their "crazy" because I'm above it, not willing to take it on as my problem. I'm watching their "show," not taking a lead role in it.

Do you have a sibling or a parent or friend who has totally flipped out on you? So often it's because they aren't feeling connected to you in a calm, loving way. They want to feel connected but the only way they've figured out how to do it is to yell or fight. If you can be the wiser one, if you can be aware of this possibility, you can do something to change it. You can remain calm. You can be a witness to their behavior and not fight back. You can listen for the clues that tell you what's really upsetting them.

And, you can use a trick we've found helpful in our house: I call it the "cactus intervention." We have a magnet on our fridge with a drawing of a sad cactus on it. Below the cute cactus is, "Hugs?" Now, who wants to hug a *cactus*? Not me. But when you're acting like a cactus (prickly and sharp) that's usually the time that you need hugs the most. Remember what I said about hurt people hurting people? Well, if you bump into a cactus it's going to hurt. If you follow the logic that the cactus itself is in pain, what does someone who is in pain need most? Love. A hug. So, how does this "cactus intervention" apply at my house? If someone is acting crabby and sharp (like a cactus) we are supposed to say, "hugs?" to let them know that we get that they might need some love but they just aren't asking for it in the right way. Make sense?

To truly understand the power of presence, try this next exercise with a friend or family member. You won't be distracted with your mind wandering away from interactions with others. If you are capable of being fully present with a friend or family member at the level described in the following exercise, not only will your need for connection be met with abundance, but the confidence and comfort in being connected at this level will carry over to your other circumstances, allowing you to feel more at peace and more confident. This energy will naturally attract other people to you in a positive way. And that's what we really want anyway, isn't it.

Exercise

The next time you're hanging out with a friend, make your entire focus what they are saying and feeling. Put your phone away. Tune out the television or music in the background. Notice their eye color. Pick a facial feature that makes them stand out and call it to mind. Listen to their words and their tone. Ask meaningful questions. Pause slightly before you speak so it's clear that your responses aren't rushed or pre-planned. Try to tune into what they are feeling and actually feel the emotions rise up in you, too. Be free with your smiles. Make as much eye contact as possible (without being creepy and stalker-like). If it's okay in the relationship, use touch (a hand on their hand or shoulder or knee) to indicate that you care and understand. Make it your primary mission to make them feel like they are at the center of your universe (again, without the bug-eyes that make them want to call the cops because you're freaking them out...all things in moderation and subtlety). ☺

What is it about this exercise that is so powerful? It opens the door to a more real level of connection. It allows you the space to be totally *with* another person. Your entire physical being is involved. You aren't scanning the room for the next thing you have to do, checking the score on TV, looking at your phone; you are completely *with* the other person.

This is *presence*.

And we know instinctively that feeling connected brings joy into a relationship. So what is the problem? We don't take the time.

Sometimes, it's just as simple as that. The shortest distance between two points is a straight line. And often the simplest answer is the right one.

If you wonder what being *present* feels like, the next time you're spending time with someone you care about, pause for a moment and notice if you're thinking about when dinner will be ready, or reaching for your phone, or even what witty remark you're going to say next. Being present truly means indulging in the joy of the moment you are in with the person you are with and not contemplating past or future events. You're giving yourself openly and completely to the person with you. There is nothing more precious.

Most of us find ourselves not being present because we're under the illusion that we're too busy. I work with my clients on time management issues so that they can fit in all of their activities into a narrow band of time. They want to know how to multi-task, and live in their over-scheduled days without consequence. I give them all that I can in the way of tools, but being present and in deep connection with others surely gets lost in that shuffle.

~Commit a Minute~

"I don't know how it gets better than this.
You take my hand and drag me head first, fearless." ~ Taylor Swift

Using the exercise above as inspiration, commit a minute, maybe five, to being completely present with each of your friends and family members. Shut out the world and make them the full focus of your attention. We talk about wanting to be the center of someone's world. That's cool, but in order to be wholly present with someone, you must make them your <u>entire</u> world for those precious moments. There can be *nothing* else. No mind wanderings. No competing desires ("I'm hungry." "I need a nap."). No distractions. Just you and the other person. Isn't your happiness worth a minute? Or five?

~*Walls and Being Disconnected*~

What if you do this and you realize that you don't enjoy being (or can't get) connected to your friend or family member or love interest? Sigh. This is why you might avoid this altogether. What if you try, and you find out that the problem is not that you're too busy for your relationship, but you're too busy because you don't want to be *in* your relationship? To be true to who you really are and were meant to be, sadly enough, you may have to face this ugly truth. Sooner or later. Because you know, deep down inside, that avoiding this truth is tying you to the person you *thought you were*, not the person you *really are* or want to become. You might have to stop pretending.

The walls we build in our relationships protect us from being hurt, disappointed, rejected, and embarrassed. We feel safe. One of the greatest problems with these walls is that they not only keep other people out, but they keep us in. When I am invested in keeping up my defenses, the "real" me cannot come out.

~*Bullies*~

The Academy Award for the most intimidating and strong walls goes to.....drumroll, please....BULLIES. Most people get so thrown off and hurt and scared by bullies that we miss the truth about them: They are filled with more fear, sadness, and insecurity than anyone. They only feel safe when they are in control of other people. They push you around so that they can feel okay about themselves and they don't have to look at who they really are because the focus is on what's wrong with *you*.

Instead of feeling fearful and rejected, feel pity for them. They are living behind walls and defenses to protect themselves from being seen because they are riddled with insecurity. It's hard to see this sometimes since they seem so sure and so tough but that's just a front: Hurt people hurt people. I think I say that three times in this book because it deserves repeating. If you're happy with yourself you aren't mean to other people. Bullies don't feel good about themselves or they would be nice to people, not mean. It's really that simple. They want to feel connected to other people just like you do, only they are going about it in a really unhealthy way. They feel "connected" by feeling in charge, watching you react to their bullying. If you don't react, they don't get their need met, so don't react. Yeah, I know, it's not quite that easy. It's also not impossible. And my approach is a whole lot better than feeling like a victim so maybe you want to give it a shot. Maybe? And reach out to a trusted adult. I can't speak for all of us, but most of us are super aware of the hurting that bullying creates and we want to help stop it. And strengthen you to withstand or stand up to it. Don't suffer in silence. Part of being in control is knowing when and how to ask for help.

~Mismatched Needs~

Obvious issues arise when you want more connection than another person does. There's that unmet need rearing its ugly head. That itching, draining, distracting, aching, and consuming need for something you don't have. You want them to be *your* definition of "close," and they don't want that. Or their definition differs from yours. Maybe you have romantic feelings for them and they just want to be "friends." Or you want to be best friends and spend a ton of time with them and they are cool being just regular, old friends. They might not even see the difference unless you push your agenda. See, they are happy where they are. Their need is being met. They have enough closeness. They don't require anything more to be satiated. But you do. Sure as the air you breathe, you need more closeness. You want to feel seen, known, and connected to on a deeper level. So there is a disconnect, a gap. An unmet need. And it's yours. And it's screaming to be filled.

You might actually feel it in your body. It might give you a hollow feeling. It might fill you with sadness. Or anger. It might make you feel numb or cold. It might show up in a disease or disorder. Studies have shown that stress has a direct impact on our physical health. Mental and emotional health affect physical health, just like the reverse. When you feel sick or in pain, your mental and emotional health is affected. You now have three of the four pillars (emotional, physical, mental, spiritual) of a solid human foundation threatened. The only one left is spiritual, and if the need is deep and consuming enough, you're probably doing some damage there, too. You're doubting if your "God" is really out there because you're in so much pain.

~For Dating Teens~

A guy I once loved when I was in high school showed me all about this "have" and "have not" struggle. Everything I described above was our relationship in a nutshell. I wanted him to want what I wanted, to need what I needed. He was interested in hooking up with me and making sure I didn't have another boyfriend, but he wasn't interested in being my legit boyfriend. Everyone knew he was keeping me hanging on so guys steered clear of me, but girls seemed to flock to him anyway. Nice, right? He was never going to feed my needs. Never. Ever. But he was so charming that every time I got to the point of moving on, he sucked me right back in.

I thought we could find a middle ground and be together. I dreamed that, someday, he would be enough for me, and I wouldn't be too much for him. And he let me think that. He dragged me along for years because I was meeting his shallow need for connection. He didn't want to let me go, but he had no intention of ever coming back to give to me the connection that I needed. It took me years to totally move on.

If you find yourself in a relationship like that, where your need for connection is different, you have a choice to make: Lower your standard (good luck with that), plan to get it met elsewhere (hobbies, other relationships), or walk. Easier said than done, I know. But how long are you going to starve (or, if you're on the other side of the equation, feel like you're a horrible person)?

Life's pretty short and in my worldview, it's not about suffering (or causing the suffering of others). It's about owning your own needs. About identifying what you need and making no apologies for it. You aren't sharing a cocoon; you have your own. You are *you* and everybody else is *everybody else*. And if you're going to spread those beautiful wings and fly, you can't do it if you don't take responsibility for who *you* are and what *you* need.

> "To live is the rarest thing in the world.
> Most people exist, that is all." ~ Oscar Wilde

Over and over again in my life I've been in relationships with people (okay, men), who were hiding their hearts. Locked away in an emotional and spiritual prison. Some were stuck in this place temporarily, while for others it seemed like a way of life. At some early point in life, I received the message that it was my job to bring healing to others.

It's an inspirational purpose, really, but the problem was that I was supposed to overcome their objections to receiving the help I was so energetically offering to them. I became an emotional Sumo wrestler cross-bred with an energetic lawyer. I would try to *love* them out of their stuck state, and deliver convincing (at least to me!) arguments on why letting their guard down with me was like winning the lottery. *"Get over her! I'll help! She broke your heart. I won't!"* They didn't buy it. I had not only failed to bring happiness and connection to my life, but to theirs as well. One painful "failure" stood on the shoulders of the one before, making me sadder and sadder.

It's no small wonder that we build walls to insulate us from connection! We believe, even if we do so subconsciously, that if we are not connected that we won't feel loss and pain. Nothing could be further from the truth. Because behind those walls we've built, there is a constant reminder of the original loss and pain. We keep the walls intact by re-living those hurts in our minds and hearts. We experience the pain over and over again to convince ourselves and others why we keep the walls intact. And we use technology (texting, social media) to hide, too. We reveal ourselves at one level by typing and posting all sorts of things, but we are missing the boat at the same time. I'm much more likely to type something and hit "send" than I am to say those same words face-to-face. Bad or good. And that causes all *sorts* of problems and frustrations.

Why is there so much angst in our personal relationships? It's simple. Fear.

~Tackle Fear~

Fear cripples us. Fear erodes trust. Trust in others, in the world at large, in our faith, and in ourselves. This lack of trust paralyzes us and, for some, fosters intense feelings of anger and hopelessness. Relationships based on mistrust, fear, anger, hopelessness, and other negative emotions bring us further and further away from living passionate and happy lives. There is no room for being authentic, and without that, we stop being real people.

I struggled for years with a deep fear and lack of trust in everything and everyone. I had what I call a "colorful" upbringing and I was deeply scarred in places. I felt abandoned and craved connection. I would rush into and then cling to relationships that nearly destroyed me on every level. Regardless of who my lover was, the relationships eventually broke apart. I didn't trust anyone, especially not myself.

What did I do to attempt to bring some calm and relief to myself? I tried to control every aspect that I could: Every word I said, how I looked, what I accomplished, and anything I could figure out that would make me feel safer within the relationship.

Did this help? Indeed. It calmed some of the fear and increased some of the trust because less was left to chance. All I offered, though, was desperate love and that was pretty pathetic. Love without trust and love polluted by fear is a sad excuse for love. Speaking of sad excuses for love, let me introduce the "fear monster."

~Fear Monster~

In college, I met this funny, smart, cute guy right before winter break. We clicked immediately, finishing each other's sentences and laughing until our sides hurt. There was a strong attraction, too, and we could talk for hours about all sorts of subjects. It felt like it was meant to be. He was graduating at the end of the semester so our relationship was fast and intense, like we were in some race to squeeze in all the great times before we had to be separated.

As we were packing up, he freaked. I mean, completely freaked out. He went from not being able to get enough of me to avoiding me like the plague. It hurt. When we finally talked, he introduced me to a concept that I'll never forget: The Fear Monster. A girl broke his heart a few years before and he was petrified that if he got too close to me that I might dump him, too. He dealt with feeling not in control (because he's not in control of what *I* do) by rejecting me before I could reject him (*him* being in control).

He was pretty aware of what he was doing and why. He called this "beast" The Fear Monster and it was in charge of what this guy did in relationships with women. Pretty sad, if you think about it. Okay, scary, since it IS a *monster*.

This whole experience sucked for me. What did I learn from it (aside from identifying the need to seek some therapy so I could see a train wreck like him coming from a mile away next time)? That there is a clear and solid connection between fear and trust and the need to have control. Relationship building is really the only thing that can reduce fear, increase trust, and invite a reduction of controlling behaviors. When people are in positive, healthy relationships, trust increases and fear decreases. As a direct result, control can lessen. Over the years, I found this same dance existing in both personal and professional settings and knew it was time to develop a model that I could use to illustrate it. Here it is:

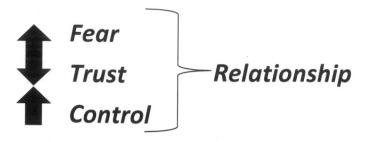

Dr. Bridget Cooper, Pieces In Place, 2013

When people feel afraid (Fear) they aren't likely to relax (Trust) and, instead, they will want to be in charge (Control) anything they can. If your parents think you might be in danger (Fear) with a certain set of friends (Trust), they might not let you go out (Control). You can also see this work with the weather. When a big storm is coming, people race to the store to get milk, bread, and toilet paper. Why? Because they are afraid (Fear) that they'll lose power or the ability to get out of their houses (Trust) so they want to do anything they can (Control) to be okay. Get it?

Take peer pressure, for instance. If you think that you're going to be left out or teased (Fear), you aren't likely to think your friends will stick by you (Trust), so you do everything you can (Control) to fit in (clothes you buy, way you wear your hair, etc.). When you're feeling anxious, take this as a neon-flashing sign that you're feeling fear because you aren't trusting that one (or more) of your needs are going to be met. Aside from trying to gain more control in order to feel less anxiety (Fear), you could spend your energy getting better connected to the people who you feel less trust with. Get it? More on this in the "Control" chapter...

~Influence It~

So the big question is, what can you do with this model? What can you do with your relationships that will have a positive impact on the mixture of fear, trust, and control? The biggest shift is that we need to start with a relationship (not a content) focus when we have conversations with others. What do I mean by a relationship (vs. content) focus?

Let's say you're on a phone call with someone and the person on the other end of the phone is completely wrong about something. Like, 100% wrong. A content-focused response would be to point out the error and try to get the person to admit that they are wrong. A relationship-focused response would question whether or not talking about the error would put the relationship in a better or worse place? If it would make it better, the issue/error would be addressed. If it would make it worse, the issue/error would be overlooked, or at the very least, softened so that the other person left the conversation feeling valued, respected, and cared about. Again, the bottom line is the *relationship*. As the relationship builds, trust increases, fear decreases, and control mechanisms relax their stronghold.

Want to know the key to building trust and ensuring that you are met with as little resistance as possible? It's easy. Validate the other person. Resist the urge to tell the person that they "shouldn't" feel a certain way. Hold your own boundaries. Let them know that you understand why they feel the way that they feel. And allow them to feel sad or mad. It's okay for them to "feel the suck." Some things just suck and facing that is honest and it's the more courageous position. They *will* move forward in their own, sweet time. Don't get your "stuff" all wrapped up in their "stuff:" The issue is not whether or not YOU would feel that way. *They* feel that way and that's enough. Say you understand their experience, their pain. Then, and only then, attempt to share your perspective, your side of things. It's a whole lot easier to take someone's hand when you're walking beside them and lead them where you want to go than it is to face them head-on, grabbing their hands and trying to pull them toward you. Don't get into a tug-of-war or a wrestling match if you want the relationship to work. Instead, see the world from their perspective for a minute, no matter how wrong you think they might be. Shhhh....you might even teach them something....

~Check Your Big, Bad Self~

What's at the core of most arguments and disagreements? Unmet needs, right? So, what brings those unmet needs to the stage, demanding attention and satisfaction? *Ego.* You know, that sense of yourself that you carry around. Your self-image that needs support and stroking in order not to collapse onto itself. Everyone has one, even those "selfless" people who seem to be doing things for other people out of the goodness of their hearts. They still have needs and they want them filled, whether they admit it outright or not.

So, if we all have egos and egos are at the core of all conflict because it's egos that are demanding one way or another that someone meet their needs, how can we reduce conflict? If you haven't noticed, I don't ask questions that I don't have the answers to. I'm tricky like that. I'll lay it out for you in this next example.

Example. I Called It! A number of years ago, I was spending time with a family of friends on Thanksgiving. My friend and her three kids (two girls and a boy) were super excited to spend time with their aunt and uncle who had just had a baby. When it came for the seats at the table to be assigned, all hell broke loose. The girls were both intent on sitting next to their aunt (and therefore, the baby) but there was only one seat open since her husband was sitting next to her on the other side. The older sister was picked and you can guess what happened next: The younger sister ran out of the room and stormed upstairs to pout about the injustice. She was mad. And sad.

The older sister came to me and told me what was going on and asked me to help. We spent a few minutes discussing the situation and she said things like, "She just needs to get over it. There's only one seat. It was going to be unfair to someone. She's being a big baby. It's not my fault. I really want to sit next to Auntie, too." And much of this she'd already said to her sister which probably accounted for her running upstairs and hiding out, ticked off.

I asked the older sister a very simple question: "What would you feel like if you hadn't been picked to sit next to your aunt?" She sighed and said, "Bad. I'd be mad and sad and feel like it was totally unfair." Well, that's *exactly* what her sister was feeling. The problem was that the older sister wanted her to stop feeling that stuff and "get over it" so she was doing what most of us naturally do which is try to talk a person out of feeling how they feel. "Don't worry." "It's going to be fine." All these phrases are aimed at making people feel better but what they really do is make the person feel like you don't think they have a right to feel how they're feeling (worried, sad, mad, etc.).

And how does that usually go when you do that and you're in a fight situation? Badly, right? Because if someone is telling you you're wrong for feeling a certain way, what is the first thing you're going to do? You're going to work hard to convince them that they're wrong and you're right and you're going to dig your heels in harder and fight.

What if instead you put yourself in their shoes for a minute and told them that you'd probably feel like they're feeling if you were them? Do you think that might work to open their ears and invite them to pay more attention to what you're saying and knock down their guard a little bit? You bet. And that's exactly what the older sister did, too. And it worked. She told her sister that if places were switched that she'd be mad and sad, too, and that she totally understood why she felt it was unfair, because there weren't enough seats to go around to make everyone happy. So, they agreed to switch off between dinner and dessert, to make it a little more fair. And Thanksgiving went off without a hitch from that point forward.

So, what's the step-by-step process to use this yourself?

1. Take a breath (or 50) and refuse to react in the heat of the moment when someone is ticked off at you. Things <u>never</u> end well that way!
2. Ask yourself why might the other person be getting pissed at you? And, "because he/she is a jerk!" is not an acceptable answer. You might be right, but try figuring out what *need* they might be trying to feed (what they might be lacking) with their obnoxious behavior. Grown people can turn into 3-year-olds when they aren't getting their needs met.

3.   Pretend your ego is the pen in your pocket or the phone in your hand and *put it away*, vowing to take it back out once the tough conversation is over. Doing this symbolic step is reminding you that if you make it about *you* and *your ego* (being "right") you may trash the relationship.

4.   Then, and only then, can you start talking to the other person. Concentrate on listening without defending. Place yourself in the other person's shoes and imagine how they might feel (again, "like the jerk that they are" is not an okay response). The goal is to focus on making the relationship better by the end of the conversation.

5.   As the conversation goes on, focus on controlling what you can (your behavior) and releasing what you cannot (their response to you). If they get nasty, you can rise above unless you want to be just like them and lose your self-respect. And recognize one thing: In a personal relationship you might be able to both get your needs met simultaneously, but don't bank on it. Like a good game of pretty much anything, take turns.

Bottom line: In order to improve the situation, you have to focus on the connection with the other person. It's all in the connection. We take risks with those we feel connected to and trusting toward. Want better relationships? Get and stay more connected. Focus on building your relationships instead of destroying them. Ask yourself what you could do to create more trust in your relationships. Listen more. Not just to the words the other person is saying, but to the messages they are trying to deliver. Are they hurt? Sad? Mad? Fearful? Resist the urge to   prove that you're right, even if you are. Put your energy into making the other person feel good (heard, understood, cared about).

Once a person starts to trust you more, they will fear less and let go of some of their efforts to be in charge of everything. If you try to convince them to trust you more or fear things less, your words will fall on deaf ears. You must *show* them that they would be right to trust you more and to let go of some of their fear. You can't try to take away control by wrestling them down for it. If you do, they will just find new ways to grab ahold of control because when you are in a state of fear and distrust, you will go to any lengths to control something, or risk going crazy.

Think you could do that? It gets easier every time you do it, I promise. And the results are amazing.

~*Master Focus*~

What does your connection to what you do have to do with focus? It's pretty simple, really. When we feel more connected to what we're doing, we are more apt to focus squarely on what's in front of us. Connection brings energy, and harnessed energy is focus. Conversely, when we are focused, we feel more connected to whatever it is that we are doing. We have eliminated distractions that keep us from feeling connected. When we focus, we connect. When we connect, we focus.

What about these "distractions?" When you're unhappy in one aspect of your life (home, school, peer relationships), you're likely to pour yourself into a hobby or a relationship, or maybe something more destructive like drugs or alcohol. You're driven to find a distraction from the lack of connection you feel, so you replace the connection. It takes you away from the true pain of the unmet need and you try to fill the hole elsewhere.

If your parents are fighting, or generally getting on your last nerve, you're likely to either make your room into a cave to get away from them or you'll spend as much time out of the house as possible, seeking attention and an escape. There's nothing tragically wrong with either one of these replacements. The need (connection, a feeling of safety and comfort) doesn't really get fed because it's the square peg to round hole issue (you're not fixing the problem, instead focusing on something else) but it does provide the needed distraction, at least temporarily. It's like snacking on a rice cake when you really want a piece of that leftover birthday cake. It just doesn't work in the end. You're still distracted by your desire for the cake. So you're not enjoying the rice cake and you're certainly not enjoying the real cake. Your attention is spread thin so you're neither here nor there.

Want the truth, though? If you eat a rice cake you won't starve. If there's no real solution (example: your parents are hell-bent on fighting and your voice isn't heard), looking elsewhere might be the best option. Please don't confuse this with permission or support for resorting to drugs, alcohol, promiscuity, gambling, violence, or self-injurious behaviors. Those are *never* the answer, despite their allure. Bottom line: Focus on what you *can* do and let go of the rest. More about that in the Control chapter.

So, what can you do to be less scattered as you attempt to get your need for connection met? You have to start with being fully in <u>one</u> moment at a time. Stress is at its height when you're chasing every bright, shiny object around because your energy is frenetic and not calm. What can you do? Focus. Get focused on what you're doing when you're doing it. How can you get more focused? In the following pages, you'll learn these sure-fire strategies to improve your focus exponentially in no time at all:

- Turn It Off
- Act Now
- End Multitasking
- Stop, Center, & Move
- Take 15

~*Turn It Off*~

My life's work is to join with people on their journeys and help them figure out their purpose in life. Bottom line: I help people change their lives. I boil my purpose on this planet into three powerful words: guide, inspire, and connect. Instead of "connect" I used to say "love," but that word is so general and overused. We "love" in so many ways, and for me, it's the connection with another human being that gives meaning to my existence. Caring about someone from a distance is nice, but without more connection, it rings hollow. And, it's through the connection that I am able to guide and to inspire. Without it, it's just words on a sheet of paper.

And that's a danger of our electronic age. We are fast forgetting how to connect. How many times have you seen a table full of "friends" who are texting or doing something else on their phones and not even looking at each other? How connected do you think the people at the table feel to one another? How about to the people they are texting? Is that really the deep connection that you are looking for?

Chances are, it leaves you feeling empty and like you are floating through life, not firmly at the wheel. I liken it to clouds. You exist in a world full of wispy, clustered clouds that spread and move without notice. And tiptoeing through life like that isn't for me. Is it for you? Personally, I'd rather be a thickly collected mass of a storm cloud, whose borders are sharp and distinct. Whose formation is noticeable and one that people stop and observe. And, whose presence is impactful, powerful, and sometimes even noisy. That's living out loud. And connected.

The next time you're paying more attention to someone or something that isn't even there, stop yourself. Take a deep breath and be where you are and with whom you're sharing oxygen. Be present. What will happen? Trust will build. Fear will dissipate. The relationship will improve. And control will stop being such a noose around your neck.

~Study Tip~

Be honest, I'm not your mom, you can tell me….how often do you have your phone out, television on, video playing when you're supposed to be studying? I walked in on my teen daughter the other day to find her quickly closing out a new online game center and diving back into her English paper assignment. Yeah, I was a teenager once and I've been caught a time or two (or a hundred) doing what I wasn't supposed to be doing when I wasn't supposed to be doing it. The only difference, really, is that I didn't have the same number of electronic distractions when I was younger. We didn't even have an *internet* (GASP!!!). The time right after dinosaurs and all that...But, I digress.

My daughter, with easy access to a game page, wasn't really focusing on her English assignment, was she? No way. If you want to give your best to your homework so you can get the best grades possible, you've got to use your desire to connect to actually give you focus. You're more powerful and intelligent than you've probably ever given yourself credit for. How do I know that? It's because when people give their full focus to something they are able to accomplish so, so much more. And that's usually more than they've ever seen themselves do, which is pretty incredible! I know I risk blowing your mind when I say that you have such untapped potential that can be popped wide open if you can focus.

So how do you get this superhero-level focus? Put away the technology. Turn off your phone, even if it's for 30 minutes at a time. Then take a 5-10 minute break and check your messages. Then turn it back off and repeat that cycle. It's okay to take breaks and to want to be in touch with others or to lose yourself in a game. That's totally cool. What isn't cool is giving half of your distracted brain to an assignment and hope that it all turns out okay and you get a good (or passing) grade. You can have the best of both worlds, you really can. I don't want you to "suffer;" trust me! I'm the most distractible person I know so I have a ton of compassion! Connect with your friends and your games and your interests by giving them 100% of your attention, just like you're giving your school work 100% of your attention. One at a time, please. ☺

~Act Now ~

Act now. Sounds easy enough, so why does it seem so hard for so many of us? Countless people complain that procrastination is their "issue." Since I'm curious by nature, I end up asking a lot of questions to find out *why* they are procrastinating. I don't get stuck in the "how" of how not to procrastinate. I need to know the "why." The "why" is what drives us, toward or away, from a destination. So, why? Why are you wanting to avoid a task? Do you have the tools, resources, skills, information you need? Do you lack confidence? Do you simply not enjoy it? Why has it become a monkey on your back?

Example. Mr. Lazy. One of my clients says he has no motivation to get things done. He starts and stops on his path to completing his goals. He gets energized, then quickly comatose. This pattern has sharply limited his ability to reach his full potential. And that's true not only because he hasn't reached the goals he set, but more so because he feels like crap about himself.

We spent some time digging around in figuring out the "why" he has for procrastinating. To get to that, I had to find out what motivated him, what brought him alive and made him feel excited. For him, it was spending time interacting with and helping others. That sounded easy enough, only he worked independently without co-workers. He had to work harder to add social connections into his daily routine. When he did, though, he found that he was on fire and blew through his to-do list. When he feels isolated, however, he finds himself with a pile of things to do and no time to get them done. Bottom line: When he attended to his need for connection, he stopped procrastinating. That was his "why." It was a need that wasn't met that was the root of the problem. Procrastination was just a symptom.

What was the disease that procrastination was a symptom of? Isolation. What does isolation indicate? A loss of connection. A lack of attention. It's easiest to see this if we consider little kids trying to meet their need for attention. What happens when we ignore little kids? When we don't meet their need for attention, love, and affection? Do they act out? You bet they do. And then we give them attention. And we criticize them because they are getting "negative" attention. We call them "trouble makers."

Truth is, they are getting attention. They are masters at finding a way to get at least part of their core need for attention met. And what do we tell them? We say that if they need attention (the good kind), to just ask instead of acting out so that they get in trouble. And if we pause for a moment in all the conflict, we can see this in ourselves, too. We're all just big kids, anyway, no matter what our chronological age is.

Why can't we see how we "act out" by failing at things that we could succeed at? Time, habit, and disappointment will do that. The role of this book is to take a tour through your core needs and determine how to attend to them and meet them and stop ignoring them. You, like any person of any age, will find a way to act out if your needs remain unmet and the outcomes are not very pretty.

Getting back to my client's story: Is he right to call himself a "procrastinator?" Absolutely not. No more so than we are right to call our kids "trouble makers." You're seeing the symptom (trouble making and procrastination) as the problem (unmet need for connection). Treat the problem (the unmet need), not the symptom (the acting out behavior). If you're getting headaches because you have a pinched nerve, does taking pain killers solve your problem? Nope. It just relieves your pain temporarily. Getting treatment to repair the pinched nerve is how you solve the problem.

So, how does my client stop procrastinating? Once he recognizes that the symptom is not the problem, he can fix both. Practically speaking, he now intentionally schedules regular meetings with *people*. In other words, feed the need and ease the pain. He won't procrastinate to create a crisis if he is getting his need met to connect with people. He won't need the drama. And he will feel invigorated by having his need met so he'll plow through his to-do list. And this isn't a prediction. It's a certainty. It worked. It works. Try it the next time you've got a project or chore you're avoiding. See how you could modify some part of it so that you could get your needs met and still get the work done.

~End Multitasking~

When I was about to graduate from college, I visited the career center of my university to get some interview tips and tricks. The jobs

I'd gotten up to that point were part-time, just-above-minimum-wage positions and I knew I had a bunch to learn about how to land a "real" job. I went through resume-writing seminars, job search strategy workshops, and an interview preparation series. I crafted a stellar resume, applied to every job that even slightly matched my background and aspirations, and perfected my interview skills.

And, I wrote some of the world's best cover letters. In every cover letter, I wrote about the personal characteristics I possessed that would make me indispensable to any employer. And, one of them was being a "strong multi-tasker." I wasn't lying. I was just ignorant and brainwashed by all those experts out there telling me how good multitasking was. I had "sucker" written on my forehead, I swear.

I <u>could</u> juggle all sorts of things simultaneously. You <u>could</u> pull me off a task and have me jump to another and I did so with a smile on my face and a bounce in my step. Apparently, being easily distracted had become a positive trait. Or not? I have since learned, through experience, observation, and research, that multitasking is the wrong approach to accomplishing our goals. Dead wrong.

Why is it the wrong way to do things? It's the absolute wrong way to get anything accomplished because when you're multitasking, you aren't focused on *one* thing. You're spreading your focus around like dust on a shelf: It has no mass so it has no intensity so it produces weak results (and sneezing, lol).

Studies have proven that when you multitask it takes you longer to get things done and you make more errors. You're distracted from each and every thing you're doing by every other thing you're doing. You're not giving anything your full attention and concentration. Your attention is all over the place. You lack focus.

And talk about not having your senses engaged: You are splitting yourself into a bunch of pieces and expecting that the result will be like it would be if you had *all* of you focused in *one* direction. It doesn't happen like that. You have to feel and be in the moment you're in. You have to see the task at hand.

So clear your work surface, shut your phone off (yes, even the text function), close your door, and resist interruptions. Take one thing at a time and do it with all that you have and you'll reap the benefits. You'll make fewer missteps. Think of it like texting and driving: The issue with that practice is that you're not giving driving your full, focused attention when you're doing something else. You don't have two heads or two sets of eyes: you only have one. Do the number of things that equals the number of brains you have to process the information? ONE. Yeah, that should do it.

The next time you're tempted to do more than one thing at a time, hear this in your head like a recording that won't stop until you do: "STOP IT! Just STOP IT!" My other clients have found that enormously helpful. (Hah!)

Speaking of "stop," next are two tactics that really assist you in resisting the urge to multitask and support you in giving your full focus and connection to each moment are done 30 seconds and 15 minutes at a time. Read on.

~Stop, Center, Move~

We run from one moment to the next without pausing long enough to focus. We forget what we want (our intentions) to get from the experience. We just fly (or for some, float) from activity to activity, place to place, forgetting to be in the moment we are actually in. We're caught up in what just happened or anxious about what is about to happen so we miss out on the things that *are* happening. And in doing this, we miss so much. And other people don't get our total focus or the whole of us, and the world fails to benefit from our what we can give to it. One practice that my clients have found enormously helpful is something called "Stop, Center, Move" and it's a quick (30 second), three-step process for bringing your *presence* to the *present*. It goes like this:

Stop	Put the phone down, shut your mouth, halt your movement.

Center   Close your eyes, quiet your mind, call to mind your intended outcome for the moment you are about to enter.

Move   Only after you've centered and focused your attention on the present moment can you move to the next moment.

All it takes is 30 seconds. Isn't your full focus worth 30 seconds? In the next exercise you'll get to try on for size how this might work.

Exercise

You have transitions from one activity to the next all day long. Whether it is racing from class to class or getting in and out of the car, you move from one space to another constantly. And sometimes you aren't even conscious of it and that spells trouble.

When you put this book down to go to do what's next on your list, take 30 seconds for sanity. *Stop:* Stay seated or laying down and close the book. *Center:* Close your eyes, concentrate on your state of mind, and think about the activity you're headed to. What resources do you need? Where does your energy need to be? What thoughts do you need to hold? Which ones to you need to release? Only after you are taken over by a sense of calm are you allowed to proceed to the third and final step. *Move:* Carry that sense of calm and focus with you, reminding yourself of the supportive thoughts and those which are not permitted, and go to your next activity.

One clarification: When you're ready to move, make sure that the moment you're about to enter is actually consistent with the intention you just set. For example, if you've decided that you want to be calm and stay out of a fight with a friend, and picking up the phone to text or call her is your next "move," you might decide to pause for a minute (or hour or day) or two before you do that. In other words, once you've centered on your intention, you might change your movement if it's not likely to spell success.

Once you move to that next activity and it concludes, take a moment to think about how it went. Was there anything different about its process or outcome than other moments? Maybe it's something you do routinely? How was it unlike the "usual?" Could you have switched activities after you centered on your intention and had better results? Making mistakes is all part of the process, just be open to learning from them.

~Take 15~

In this distracted, technology-consumed, overwhelmed world we've created, we are rewarded for having the attention span of a squirrel. And not just any squirrel. More and more it's like we are all squirrels on crack cocaine. Pretty image, huh? Well, I don't need to remind you that the roads are littered with flattened squirrels. Why? If you watch a squirrel try to cross a road, it rarely runs with purpose and intensity from one side to the other. Instead, it gets part of the way into the street, then seemingly starts looking around for who knows what, and the next thing you know, the minivan barreling down the road just sent it to squirrel heaven.

What can you learn from the squirrels of the world (another of many things I never thought I'd hear myself say)? You can decide to move with purpose, intensity, direction, and FOCUS. Be in the moment you're in instead of the moment that promises to approach. Accept the scattered nature of our society (if you feel you must) and work within its constraints. And remember to *focus*.

One reason people don't start a project is because they can't seem to find the time. Is this you? You imagine how long it will take and you don't have four or five (or more) consecutive hours to work on it. So you don't start it. It sits. Mocks you. Gnaws at you. It fills you with guilt and self-doubt. You've failed before you even started. And chances are, you get in trouble for not doing it, whether it be a bad grade, a scolding from a parent, or losing your phone for a week (*again*). Are you ready for another way? Read on.

Imagine that you're working on a big project and you get interrupted. So you don't go right back to it, or when you do, you forgot where you left off. You forgot your place. So you have one more reason not to start it again. So you abandon it. Or procrastinate until it's crisis mode and you're really in trouble. It's the night before it's due and all hell breaks loose in your house as you scramble to get it done and still get some sleep.

There <u>has</u> to be a better way!

There *is*. You can avoid those last minute crises by handling projects better to begin with. You can handle stops and starts if you have the right techniques in place ahead of time.

Set aside reasonable blocks of time to work on a project. If you know that your attention span is, let's say, just this side of a squirrel on a sugar high, then don't block two hours for it. If you do, you'll find a hundred other things to do instead. E-mail. Laundry. Organizing your sock drawer. All of these things are good things, but they aren't what you set out to do. And they are not getting you closer to your goal. Are you tired of getting to the end of a day and feeling no closer to accomplishing your true goals than when you woke up?

Try this instead: Take on tasks 15 minutes at a time. Rather than trying to focus on a project for hours at a clip and then getting frustrated with a dozen interruptions, commit to biting off some chunk of the project for 15 minutes at a time. And do nothing (not even checking your text messages or incoming emails or phone calls) for that 15 minute block except for that project chunk. Give it your full attention. Lose yourself in it by setting an alarm that will stop you at the end of 14 minutes.

Why 14 minutes? If you leave one minute at the end of your 15 time frame, you have time to write yourself what the military coins a "pass down" (a snapshot of where you left off, what you were about to do next, and remaining steps to complete that section). Why is this necessary and why does this intervention work? When you exit and attempt to re-enter a task at a later time, you lose ground in your comprehension and planning abilities and it takes you a significant amount of time to get back to where you were before you left the task.

For example, have you ever been engrossed in a really good book, only to be interrupted and have to put it down suddenly. You're like that dog in the movie "Up" who is present to the person speaking to him one minute and then he sees a "SQUIRREL!" (What is it about squirrels, anyway?) And all of his focus was lost. It works the same for you. When you pick up the book again a day or two later you find yourself reading several pages before the page you stopped on because you need to locate your place in the story again.

It works the same way with a project you're working on, only you're the one who is responsible for writing the pages (delivering the work product). No one has done the heavy lifting for you. It's up to you to bring the brain power, inspiration, and focus to the project or task. If you don't know what you were thinking when you stopped mid-stream, you'll be forced to review what you've done and hope that you can figure out where you left off and where to go from there.

Instead, hit a virtual "pause button." Leave yourself a "pass down" reminder so that you can skip that frustrating, time-consuming, and useless step and instead get right back to business. A "pass down" reminder should be brief, easy to comprehend, and directed at positioning your mind to be exactly where it was when you walked away. A good way to write a good "pass down" is to imagine that you ran off to that Caribbean getaway you keep dreaming of and your body double needs to jump right in and make it happen. What would you tell him to do next? Just a couple of quick guiding statements are necessary. Since I'm all about the implementation, I'm going to offer testimony to it along with giving you the nuts and bolts.

When I was writing my dissertation in pursuit of my doctorate, I needed all the help I could get. For those of you who are unfamiliar with a dissertation, it's basically a book (mine was 374 pages long). More specifically, it is a research proposal followed by a description of the research project and research results. It has to be reviewed painstakingly by your academic advisor and a committee of professors and professionals. It puts your academic muscles to the stretch test, even under the best of circumstances.

Well, with a baby and a toddler in tow was clearly not the best of circumstances. My youngest was still needing my round-the-clock attention. Thanks, kid (not!). I believe that she was regressing because I was being pulled in other directions and she was having none of it. She hasn't changed much since, her hair just got longer and her vocabulary more extensive. And my three-year-old was full of her own challenges. She needed Mommy, too, so I was scatterbrained to say the very least.

Oh, and did I mention that I was running my own business out of my house and writing a dissertation while taking care of my daughters? Insanity. Bottom line: If this focus approach worked for me, it sure as heck will work for you.

Every time I had to put my dissertation down to attend to something else, I left myself a note ("pass down") right there in the document stating what I was about to start working on, what I was thinking, and the next couple of things I wanted to look at. It took all of about 60 seconds, which was tolerable to my little ones (well, some moments more than others). When I returned to the computer, I was able to pick up where I left off and move forward.

As a result, the interruptions didn't cost me much time. And that was critical given how often I got interrupted and taken off my task. And I was a more relaxed mom because I knew that focusing on my children wasn't going to make things go badly for me and cause me additional work. Well, at least that was true when I remembered to hit "save changes," but that's another story altogether.

In addition to the "pass down" approach, the other saving grace in tackling that mountain of a project was breaking things down into manageable chunks. When I thought about writing 300-400 pages on a topic, I wanted to hide under a rock. It was more than nerve-wracking. It was downright terrifying. I had to find a way: First, to motivate myself to first come out from hiding, and second, to actually write it. So I analyzed the project and divided it into chapters (each had an electronic folder) and chapter sections (each had a separate document). Then, every time I got time to write, I'd open up a folder then a document. In order to finish that document I might only have 3-8 pages to write. That wasn't so terrible. After I completed each document in a chapter, I folded the documents into one. Can I tell you how much easier all of this made it for me to *focus*?!

After not too long, I had hundreds of pages written and my project was nearing completion! If I had created a document called "dissertation" knowing it needed to be hundreds of pages long once I'd finished, seeing a blank "page 1 of 1" staring back at me would have driven me to quit before I started. Equipped with this solid approach, I kept going. I finished. In record time, too.

Convinced yet? Try it out. Give it a chance and you won't be disappointed. Promise.

~The Power of Now~

"It's something unpredictable, but in the end it's right.
I hope you had the time of your life." ~ Green Day

I am going to wrap up this chapter and stand on my soapbox for a minute to make a point that deserves your full attention, and it has something to do with my license plate. Yes, my license plate. I decided to get one of those specialty plates and here's what it says: JUST BE.

I cannot begin to tell you how many smiles and positive comments I get from people when they read it. And from these impromptu interactions and conversations I get one clear message: We lose sight of being in the here and now.

So, what's my soapbox message?

Be *present.*

Be IN the present moment. Too many of us are in another moment than the moment we are in....wishing it away and distracted by a moment not yet arrived, just to do the same to that moment once we get *there*. Live in the moment you're in. Focus on it deeply. Focus brings passion, effectiveness, and accuracy to each project. It brings an intensity that drives us to accomplish things we never thought possible. When we are in the right now, only wanting now, we appreciate it with all of our senses. We embrace its power. We notice things we would otherwise ignore. We are completely *present*. We don't long for the past or wish for the future. All we want is now.

That kind of focus is powerful. Pinch your arm, be aware of your breathing, say the word "focus." Whatever it takes. People want to be with people who are present and connected to them because it's rare to find someone who is like that. Don't you want to be special and rare?

Researchers say that we only use a small portion of our brain. What if we could tap into more of its potential? Look at what you accomplish on a daily or weekly basis. View it not only in terms of breadth (variety of activities) but depth (how deeply and expertly you tackle a task). Imagine if you could tap into your full potential of focus and connection in each moment? If you could bring the totality of YOU to each encounter? Give your experiences the fullness of your mind, body, and spirit. It's awe inspiring, really. And intense. And completely possible.

Now multiply that. Imagine if more people joined you in bringing their full selves and all of their senses to every interaction. What would that produce? I'd be lying if I said I didn't spend time imagining our world with more connection, more presence, and more intensity. When I was a little kid, I contemplated a nirvana-like world and honestly believed that I was going to have a hand in creating it. I was young, naïve, and full of odd notions, for sure. Yet, more than 30 years later, I still have whispers of those images in my head.

I believe, now more than ever, that we create our own world, regardless of our age or circumstances in life. We make our experiences. We decide what we want, what we will tolerate, and how we will seek to meet our needs. We are in charge of how we plug into this world and how much we invest in each moment. If we simply make more thoughtful choices over and over again, we can create the world (or at least our corner of it) in our image. It's what we've done to this point: Created a world in our image. Maybe it's high time we shift our self-image. Make it a little more positive (not delusional), powerful (not power-mongering), and compassionate (not gullible). Wishful thinking? Perhaps. Change starts with me. And, with you.

"Be the change you want to see in the world."
~ Mahatma Gandhi

Connection & Presence

~End of Chapter Inventory~

"Not all of us can do great things. But we can do
small things with great love." ~ Mother Teresa

Summary: To address how the need for connection drives us and
is at the core of most emotional and relational issues.

Key Concepts:

- Of all of the needs, the need for connection is the most central,
  but the levels of need differ and cause problems
- Being more connected takes work and being present, which
  requires focus, as well as facing fear head-on.
- Some of the strategies for being focused include: Act Now;
  End Multitasking; Stop, Center, & Move; and Take 15.
- There is tremendous power in the NOW.

What are three takeaways you have from this chapter? What
did you learn about yourself and/or others? What shifts in thinking did
you experience as a result of reading this chapter?

Takeaway 1:

Takeaway 2:

Takeaway 3:

Rate yourself on your confidence and competence practicing the key concepts in this chapter:

1: I'm so lousy I don't want to respond

2

3

4

5: I'm okay, but I have a lot to learn

6

7

8

9

10: I'm going to write my own book on this competency

What are three things you commit to do (differently) as a result of reading this chapter? Think of things that will improve your life personally, spiritually, emotionally, and physically.

Commitment 1:

Commitment 2:

Commitment 3:

What are three roadblocks and challenges to being where you need to be? In other words, what are three things (relationships, habits, assumptions, situations) that you need to adjust and/or remove in order to live happier?

Roadblock 1:

Roadblock 2:

Roadblock 3:

What are three strategies for addressing those roadblocks and challenges? What are three changes you could make that would reduce or remove the obstacles you have?

Strategy 1:

Strategy 2:

Strategy 3:

"I've learned that people will forget what you said, people will
forget what you did, but people will never forget
how you made them feel." ~ Maya Angelou

5

CONTROL

"All the art of living lies in the fine mingling of
letting go and holding on." ~ Havelock Ellis

Control isn't black or white. Control is on a continuum. Control is one of those words that sometimes is met with displeasure, and sometimes with a high five. When you call someone "controlling," it's usually not a compliment. Yet when you say that someone is "out of control" that's not good either. Either extreme is seen as negative. But simply being "in control" is usually met with respect and admiration.

Being a teenager, control is a touchy subject, for sure. The whole path of adolescence is moving from having someone or some people (your parent or parents) in charge of you to figuring out how to be responsibly in control of yourself. I have a secret that I'd like to share with you. And your parents may be incredibly mad at me for telling you this, so shhhhhh....

Your parents are *not* in control of you. They never have been. Ever. No one is in control of anyone else. We were born with this pesky little thing called "free will" and we use it. A lot. Or a little. When our parents tell us to do something we can listen or not. Either way, we exercise our free will when we respond. Parents (and teachers and friends and family members and society at large) have influence over us (sometimes a great deal of it), but they never have *control*. Never. You're in charge of you and you get to decide how much you want to be influenced. Intrigued? Read on.

~ Control and Environment ~

Setting has a great deal to do with our tolerance for varying levels of control. For instance, a military officer is risking the lives of his troops if he is not in control of every detail. On the other hand, you might tend to relinquish control over the little things when you're relaxing on the beach on vacation. What's the difference between those two scenarios? Aside from drinking from a canteen in one and a bright glass with a rainbow umbrella in the other, the difference is trust and fear. The military officer has lives depending on his command of and control over every element in the operation. People will die if he drops a ball. People are trusting him with their lives. And they cannot be plagued with fear or they cannot focus on their mission. They are in an environment of fear and danger, yet they must trust. So it follows that efforts toward control are high.

When you're on the beach on vacation, aside from wanting to make sure you've got a towel, sunscreen, and a cold spot to store your beverages, you can let go of control. You're there to relax and the threat of death isn't looming anywhere nearby. You don't feel much, if any, fear and you trust that things are going to be okay. So, your need to control every little detail is minimal.

Well, unless you're a control freak. If you are, as you were reading that last passage you might have even started to tremble thinking about going to the beach and not having every last element of that venture planned out, monitored, and executed. There's no such thing as "relaxing" for a control freak. If you are one, the only way that you can "relax" is if everything is in perfect order and under your direct influence.

But, be honest: That never happens to a satisfying degree so you never really relax. You're always thinking about some little thing that might have jumped the tracks that you so painstakingly laid out and what NOW? What terrible thing is lurking just around the corner that you haven't compensated for? What will happen if you can't figure it out and be in charge of its process and outcome?

On the outside you might appear completely calm, but on the inside you're about to blow a gasket. Your mind is racing and you're getting agitated trying to figure out how to regain total control over the situation.

~Fear and Control~

"Don't worry 'bout a thing.
'Cause every little thing gonna be alright." ~ Bob Marley

Where does this all come from? Your efforts to control anything and everything in your path stems from fear and distrust. You fear that people and situations won't do as you need them to do and that leads to a distrust of anything that is outside of your influence. If you're not in charge, bad things will happen. (It might help you to refer back to the Fear-Trust-Control model presented in the Connection & Presence chapter.)

If you're afraid of something (an outcome that you don't want to happen), you won't trust the situation and you'll then try to control anything and everything that you can to reduce the fear you feel. Control feels good when you have fear and don't trust because it shrinks the fear of the unknown and somehow mitigates the lack of trust. You are mastering something, at least, so your mind eases a bit.

When people are fearful, they don't trust others and they take actions to feed their need for control. Most people demand to have their needs met, including the one for control. They might not be direct about it. Most people aren't. But they will demand that you feed their needs in roundabout, manipulative, and even passive aggressive ways. And that "they" might be "you." Yes, *you.*

When you have a need that's not being filled, as we discussed earlier in this book, you WILL find a way to satisfy it, to some degree. Somehow. In a healthy way or an unhealthy way, you'll make the effort to fill it. And, of all the needs, control is the one that this applies about 100% of the time. People don't like not having some control over things. Some need it over just their own selves. Others "need" to have control over everyone and everything.

A couple of women I used to work with and I would comment when something went wrong beyond our office, "if they'd only asked us, this never would have happened." It brought a laugh, but it stemmed from this sense that if only we could be in control of more things, fewer events would go wrong. Just like that car accident that almost happened because some "crazy" driver just cut you off.

I hate to be the one to say it, but that's what makes people (especially parents) nuts about teen drivers: The adults aren't in control. I remember my mom teaching me how to drive. It's a miracle that we both survived! And I learned on a "stick shift" on Massachusetts hills and back roads. My thoughts as the TEEN: "Kill me now. Please." I can only imagine what my mother was thinking...

The fact of the matter is that regardless of how bad and inconsiderate the others drivers on the road are, you can only operate your own car. You can't drive theirs. You can be a defensive, considerate driver and not let the sometimes ridiculous moves they make affect your day. And their actions might put you in danger. They might even kill you or someone you love. But you can't drive for them. And cutting (or flipping) them off will only make things worse (ever hear of road rage?).

I'm sorry to be the one to point this sad fact out to you, but it's a fact of life (like driving): Other people will do what they want to do and you aren't in charge, no matter how ridiculous, offensive, or dangerous their actions are. How can you move through the world while embracing that? Start with figuring out how to distinguish what you *can* control and what you *can't* and shift your focus accordingly.

~*Parents: Fear & Control*~

Parents have fear just like you and me. In some ways and in certain cases, they have a boatload more of it. Why? Well, when we first became parents, we were given the immense responsibility of taking care of our babies. Our babies were completely dependent upon us so we had to maintain a great deal of control to keep them safe and healthy. As they grew, our need to control things should have dissipated as it was replaced by them needing less "help."

Yet, that's not an exact science, and it scares the daylights out of many parents. They feel safer when they feel more in control, just like anyone. When it comes to the lives of their kids, this need to feel safe by being in control is priority number one sometimes. I'm not advocating that your parents should keep trying to control you, especially since I already tipped my hand and told you that your parents really aren't in control of you anyway. I'm just suggesting that you might want to cut them some slack when they are trying to be all bossy-bossy with you.

The truth is that they are afraid, they feel anxiety, so they try to overcome this anxiety by exerting control. Instead of rebelling against them, see if you can use the Fear-Trust-Control model to build your relationship (Trust) so that they can feel less fear and let go a little. Baby steps…

~**Meeting the Need for Control**~

Meeting a need for control is often easy to do. Just identify a bunch of details to focus all of your attention on. Have at it. Honestly, that only goes so far. And it often results in cardiac disorders, ulcers, and probably some rapid weight gain or loss. There is a better way. It requires that you spend as much energy <u>holding on</u> as <u>letting go</u>. If you've ever gone waterskiing, you'll appreciate this next analogy.

When you're sitting in the water, before the boat has started to move, skis on and tips up, holding onto the rope, you're supposed to be completely relaxed and focused only on having the right posture for when you're pulled forward to stand up. When the boat starts going, you stay just as you are, letting there be a whole bunch of slack in the rope.

Only when the boat's distance from you is sufficient to take up the slack on the rope are you able to be pulled out of the water. If you're skilled enough to stand up and stay up, you are then focused on keeping the tension tight on the rope that connects you to the boat. If you allow be too much slack, you're likely to fall over since there isn't any tension to hold you up. If you hold too rigidly to the rope, any movement of the boat could toss you right off of your feet. There is a delicate balance.

The same goes for figuring out how to meet your need for control and allowing others to do the same for themselves. You have to hold on tightly yet loosen your grip simultaneously. I started learning this lesson many, many years ago. They say that a journey of a thousand miles begins with one step. More times than not, my journeys have begun with tripping and falling flat on my face. When I used to ice skate in elementary school, my trainer taught me to purposely throw myself onto the ice. Honestly, I thought she was nuts! She told me that falling was not how most skaters suffered major injuries. Instead, it was by *fighting the fall.* Resisting the inevitable. Trying to control the uncontrollable. Getting used to pain was the only way to lessen my natural fear of it.

At age nine I had no idea that she was preparing me for life. But I didn't really learn what she was trying to teach me. Okay, I learned a little of it. I'm a quick study but, like a lot of people, I seem to seek out similar situations over and over again. I always hope it's to learn the lesson so I can be free of that painful repetition, but I've come to believe it's the comfort of the familiar that draws me in again and again. The devil I know is better than the devil I don't know.

Problem is, either way, it's the devil. But my skating instructor was, in fact, giving me control over myself and my fear. She knew that the less I feared falling the less likely I would be to fight it and injure myself more. The approach I learned: To influence what I can (practice often to minimize my errors) and let the rest go (fall into the fall).

~*What Can't You Control?*~

"A pessimist sees the difficulty in every opportunity;
an optimist sees the opportunity in every difficulty."
~ Winston Churchill

So, what can you control? What are you in charge of? The list is long and comprehensive, and might even be daunting. You might be irritated that it's all about you and doesn't say a thing about all those players in your life that you'd like to "get in line." Sorry. No deal there. Maybe we should start with what you *can't* control. You <u>cannot control other people</u>. Need me to say that again? You cannot control other people. You are only in charge of *you*. And that's enough. It's a full-time job. You might even be able to use an assistant. And you know exactly what I mean. You and all of your worries and thoughts and plans and relationships and baggage: It's a lot for one person to handle. You really don't have the time to exert effort trying to control other people.

So the next time you're trying to step into someone else's "stuff" and determine what they should do and how they should do it, take a look in the mirror and check yourself: Is *your* house in order? Where are *you* letting things slip? It's true what they say about people in glass houses; They shouldn't throw stones. I have a little secret for you: We ALL live in glass houses.

A good starting point for meeting your need for control without driving yourself and others around you to the brink of insanity is to use that brain in your head to determine what you can control. This means doing a thorough inventory of what you have influence over, what you can control, and what is out of your control.

When I counseled addicts and their families years ago, we used a model with our clients to help them to work on overcoming their addiction. This model was based on control, which is interesting since once addicts got to us they were pretty much completely *out* of control. We would ask them if:

1) They were solely responsible for their thoughts, feelings, and behaviors; or,
2) Others influenced their thoughts, feelings, and behaviors; or,
3) *Both* the first and the second answers were true.

Over years of observation and experience, our team found that if they picked the first option, they failed to see the influence of others and they would likely be blindsided in their recovery when someone negatively influenced them. If they picked the second option, we saw that they failed to see their own responsibility and would not take ownership of recovery and move through and past it. But, if they picked the third option, they appreciated the blend of responsibility and influence and they had a good shot at recovery. They recognized that they could control their own thoughts, feelings, and behaviors but that others influenced those very same things. If they neglected to see that influence, they would surely relapse. And if they thought that they weren't in control of their own thoughts, feelings, and behaviors, they would never successfully address their own addiction recovery.

~Control Bucket~

What does addiction recovery have to do with you? So much. There are things that we can control about ourselves and things we can't. Aside from plastic surgery, you can't change your body type, facial features, and height. We *can* control four main categories of things, which constitutes our **control bucket**:
1) Our thoughts and interpretations
2) Our attitude
3) Our behaviors and actions
4) Our boundaries.

Now before you get frustrated because I only listed four things you can control, please see that this list is <u>immense</u>. It's a very long list that requires a great deal of attention and effort. If you're like a lot of people, though, it's missing the things you've been trying to control for as long as you can remember: Other people and events.

We cannot *control* them, but we can have an effect (*influence*) on them. The remainder of the world, events, and what people actually do with our "influence" is not in our control. At all. My advice? Focus on what you can control: **You.** What you do, think, and feel. I'm pretty sure that's enough.

When you think about people, I'm figuring that you consider all the things you'd like to be in charge of. How they feel about you. What they say about and to you. How they treat you. How they perform. How they drive. When it comes to events, you want to control tragedies, illnesses and diseases, bad luck, poor weather, stock market dives, wars, and so on.

For all of those things, there may be things you can do to influence them. You can take good care of yourself to head off health struggles. You can bring an umbrella or a coat if it's supposed to be rainy or cold. You can vote someday, write letters, protest, and stay informed if you want a voice in your country's participation in war. But you cannot *control* these things. You cannot control other people. You are only in charge of you. Only you. But *all* of you. And, trust me, that's as much as you can or want to handle.

The next bucket is things you can influence, which does include other people (their thoughts, feelings, behaviors) and circumstances. Influence is very different from control. It's the difference between inviting someone to a party and making it sound incredibly fun (influence) and kidnapping someone and bringing them to the party (control). You have a great deal of influence in a whole host of circumstances in your life, and the more you are in charge of your own "stuff," the more influence you have over others.

The four things we can *influence* (not control!) are:
1) Other people's thoughts and interpretations

2) Other people's attitudes
3) Other people's behaviors and actions
4) Other people's boundaries

Considering the party example I just gave, please realize one very important distinction: Influencing someone to bring them to the party still provides them a good time whereas forcing someone to attend doesn't mean they will stay and/or have a good time (remember free will?). Your energy and attention is much better spent on trying to *control* you and *influence* others.

~*Control Your Thoughts & Interpretations*~

Starting from the inside out, you are able to control your thoughts and interpretations. When you walk into a room, you get to decide if you'll see others as being out to undermine you OR as a roomful of potential best friends. If someone you know walks past you, you get to decide if you'll assume that they hate you or are mad at you or if they just didn't see you. **You** own your own filter. **You** choose the lens through which you see people and their actions. **You** select your own self-perception. If you don't fit into your jeans, you can see it as testimony that you're a fat slob or that you simply need to eat less and walk more.

We can use our power over our thoughts to overcome our fears and apprehensions: To seek better outcomes because we see things as *possibilities* and not *problems*. We can also use our control over our interpretations to feed our self-esteem. If we believe that others have failings but generally mean well, we can use our power over our thoughts to smooth things out. Instead of seeing their failings as judgment about who we are or what we have or haven't done, we can choose to see others as being human. You know, just like *you*.

And what follows thoughts and interpretations? Behaviors and actions.

~*Control Your Behaviors & Actions*~

You are in charge of how you act. Only you. Other people can and will influence you, but it's your choice how you behave. You get to decide how you will operate in the world. Your history may influence you, and your circle of relationships may contribute by reinforcing certain actions (what is judged acceptable or unacceptable). Decisions are your greatest control mechanism: yes vs. no; keep vs. toss; add vs. subtract; stay vs. leave; move vs. sit. If someone irritates you, you're the only one who decides how you respond. *You* decide. Only *you*. Even if there is a gun to your head, you always have a choice. Use it.

You want to feel more in control? Choose to do the opposite of whatever the person setting off your frustration expects or wants you to do. Have you ever looked affectionately at someone while they were yelling at you? If someone wants to pick a fight, you can decide to join in or walk away. Group influences are strong, for sure, but they do not control you anymore than you control other people.

We all have people in our lives who seem hell-bent on starting an argument or getting us to react in a certain way to whatever their latest drama or complaint is. They seem to know just what to say to get a reaction. There is power in that. There is power in knowing that you can puppet master another human being. It's almost like they are saying, "watch THIS." Is that what you want to be? A puppet? Doesn't the vision of them operating your strings make you want to crawl out of your own skin?

So why are you giving them that power? No one can make you do anything. If you react to them, that is you exercising your power. If you let them get to you, that is also you exercising your power. You can choose to react or to respond. When you react, it often seems unintentional. It's in the moment. It's like an impulse, something that doesn't even go through your head to be processed: You just do it. Responding is different. It might also be quick, but it travels through the brain and the spirit first. It is in full consciousness. It is intentional. It is with purpose and desire and thoughtfulness. And it is in control. In control of your behaviors and actions. This isn't easily done, especially if these people are around you constantly. It's a good time to reach out for help and support so you can manage your thoughts effectively.

Exercise

Consider the most difficult person in your life right now. On the left side of a piece of paper, write down what the most frustrating thing they do that gets under your skin. On the right side of the paper, brainstorm all of the ways that you could respond. First, jot down what you usually do. Then add other things you may have tried. Then write what someone like Mother Teresa would do. Perhaps add how a comedian might treat the situation. Be creative. Come up with at least five approaches, ten if you're ambitious. Step back. Take a look at the list. This is your list of choices. Keep this list handy. You get to choose which one of these responses you want to commit to. When you try a new approach, consider how it worked. Journal about it. Talk with a friend and share your reflections. Ponder what was good and not so good about it. And as you're thinking about it all, keep reminding yourself that you made a choice, and you always make choices. And you can choose differently next time, and maybe you'll witness a different outcome?

The moral of the story is that you are in charge of how you behave. If you're blaming others for what you're doing, stop it. Just stop it. At the end of the day, you're in charge of you. Start acting like it.

~*Control Your Attitude* ~

The next thing you are in charge of is your attitude. Depending on what kind of attitude you decide to sport, you can meet your need for control, less or more. The attitude you have affects so many things. If you are cheerful, you invite others to be the same way, as a mirror for you. When you are grouchy and complaining, others feed into that, as well, and create more of that negative energy.

If you're feeling sad but you want to have a good time, what attitude will put you more in control of that outcome? That's right: An upbeat one. It's like cancer cells: They multiply. Attitude "cells" multiply, too. Which ones do you want multiplying? The good ones or the toxic ones? Did you ever notice that the more sadness you express to others that the sadder you feel?

There was a period of my life a few years back that I was the saddest sack around. One of my very best friends actually heard me on the phone one day and her heart broke a little because I didn't even sound like myself. I was broken and getting through every day felt like a chore. I'm pretty sure I was suffering from a mild depression brought on by a love affair gone terribly and irrevocably wrong.

And my attitude brought everyone down. People looked at me and gave me that sad look, bottom lip puckered and everything. It spread like wildfire. Did it make me feel any better? Of course not. I'd made my inner experience an outward one and shared it like the plague, and it just made me sicker and sadder.

What would have happened if I'd put on a happy face, knowing that I had the sadness on the inside? Would more people have smiled at me? Might I have forgotten even for a passing moment all the reasons I had been holding onto to make me sad? You betcha. My aunt called this approach "fake it till you make it." If you pretend you're happy it won't take long for you to believe it and for the forces in the world to remind you of your blessings. So feed the sadness or feed the happy: It's all up to you.

Think of the effect you can have on not only your own life but the lives of others. It's immense. And it's control in the right way for the right reasons. You get to control what part of yourself that you put out into the world: The image you project. And that image starts on the inside so if you've got some work to do on your self-esteem, what are you waiting for?

There is no wizard of self-worth who is going to show up in your kitchen one day and say "abracadabra!" and fix you. When you're saying all those bad things to yourself, imagine hearing someone you love talking to him or herself that way. What would you say? And no, "but I'm RIGHT about ME" doesn't cut it as an excuse. You deserve love and care as much as anyone.

Your spirit believes the words you tell it. It wants to trust you and make you "happy" so it will do all that it can to prove you right. If you tell yourself that you're junk, believe you me, you will build a mountain of evidence and experiences to prove that voice right. So let's start with a great self-image example regarding attitude so you can get ahold of your thoughts that lead you to your attitude. This attitude control example concerns something that so many of us struggle with: Body image.

Example: Fat Ass Syndrome. Ever get dressed in the morning and feel like you've put on a few unwanted pounds? How is your confidence? It's in the basement. Where is your focus? Directly on your (perceived) fat ass. That's why I call it "Fat Ass Syndrome." Yes, I said "ass" in print. Let's call a spade a spade. Or an ass an ass. Please forgive the profanity. "Bottom" and "tush" are just so much less powerful in making my point. And girls may get this one quicker than guys. Feel free to replace "ass" with "gut" if that fits your body shape better, k?

What happens as you proceed through your day and face challenges and random glances from people when you feel like your ass is flabby or enormous (and not in a Kim Kardashian sort of way)? You think that everyone is looking at your fat ass. You'd swear it's actually flashing neon and making loud, swishing sounds as you walk. But chances are that no one is judging you as harshly as you're judging yourself.

Okay, so what if it's not just your voice criticizing you but it's coming from the outside, too?

His name was Mike Stanavich. I met him in high school and I'll likely never forget him. He was one of those charming, fast-talking, arrogant bad boys that every injured, low self-esteem teen girl heads for like a train wreck. Now, I was that girl but I was fortunate enough to never get involved with him. Why am I bothering to mention this guy? He was the mean, self-hating voice inside my head, in boy form. I'll never forget how it felt when he said to me one day in my freshman year in high school, "you're cute, but your ass is fat." Yeah, he did. In the hallway. It was like every horrid thing I'd ever said to myself was made true and real and known by everyone. It was awful. Thirty years later I can still remember his voice when he said it and how I felt when I heard it.

I think it's worth mentioning that at the time he said it, I'd been struggling with eating disorder behavior for at least seven years. Diet pills, laxatives, binging, purging, starvation, and every diet plan under the sun were my daily existence. It's also worth mentioning that I was 5'3" and weighed 110 pounds. My body image was so out of whack that I thought that my ass was the size of a trailer truck. After Mike's comment, I dug my heels in even further and began starving myself for weeks at a time, trying to succeed at being thinner.

What does this have to do with control? Absolutely everything. The rest of my life felt so out of control that I focused on the one thing that I felt I could control: The size and shape of my body, how much I ate, and my exercise regimen were in my control. I couldn't stop the craziness going on around me in my alcoholic and abusive home, so I focused on my body. When you try to exert control over things to compensate for the stuff that is going badly in your life you can do a great deal of damage to yourself (and others).

Eating disorders are just one of the ways that we hurt ourselves when our need for control is not met. Some teens experiment with drugs, alcohol, tobacco, and other mind-altering substances to take their minds off the crazy in their lives, to feel more in charge of something. Or they get promiscuous. The problem with any addiction (food, drugs, alcohol, tobacco, sex, etc.) is that the *addiction* is in control. Not *you*. The *addiction*. It's a fantasy world that so many of us get caught up in as we try to compensate for not feeling in control of other stuff.

For those of you wondering if Mike Stanavich and I are now friends on Facebook, the answer is no. He died in his twenties in a police chase. I mention this not because I want to smear his name but to make a point about the voices we listen to. He was a troubled and sad young man who struggled to keep his head above water in his own life.

Yet, I let that one comment from him confirm all my worst fears and set me on a path to let my eating disorders worsen and my depression deepen. I wish I could have seen him for who he was and the pain he was in. If I could have, I might have been able to hear what he said as his way of letting out some of the pain and self-hatred he had for himself, because it was abundant.

Like most bullies, he was hurting inside so he hurt others. Bullies need to feel in control of other people so they control them with their nasty words and hurtful comments and excluding behavior. Don't be fooled: The girls or guys in cliques are bullies, too. In order to be "popular" or "fit in," you have to agree to conform to what their rules are: What to wear, what to say, how to talk, who to date, etc. These bullies may be prettier and wear a smile, but a bully is anyone who seeks to control you by making you feel badly about yourself.

"Respect your haters. They're the only ones who think
you're better than them." ~ Nicki Minaj

What can you learn from this?

Focus on getting strong so you can't be controlled by someone else. Decide to hold onto your own control and not handing it to someone else. Get yourself in check and work on getting *your* mental act together. That's a huge piece of what you can control. Focus there. Focus on changing what you don't like or focus on letting it go. If you don't like how flabby you feel, go for a run or skip the ice cream next time. Stop complaining if you aren't going to do something about it. If you're doing something about it, stop complaining. Simple enough for you?

~*Control Your Boundaries*~

I'm the go-to girl with my friends when they have issues, big and small and I have been for as long as I can remember. I hear every kind of psychic struggle. The situations differ but often the core struggle is figuring out where they "end" and the other person "begins." In other words, what are their boundaries? What is in their control and what is not? How can they influence the situation and what do they need to let go of? How can they get their needs met (in this case, the one that gives them some semblance of control)?

~Crazy~

At one tumultuous point in my life, I consulted a coach to get and keep me on a grounded path. After hearing my story, she shared a concept with me that fit me like no glove ever could. When you grow up in a crazy family with caretakers who are mentally ill, you have a tragic choice to make in order to survive. Either you recognize their illness, or you believe that you are crazy to believe that your caretakers are ill. It's a choice that leaves you feeling insane either way.

If you believe the latter, you trust nothing about your own perceptions, instincts, or feelings. You know the truth (they are crazy) but you refuse to attest to it. Your subconscious mind knows better, so you've now set up a distrustful relationship with your own mind. As a result, you end up being the "crazy" one, which makes it easier on your caretakers because *you* become the problem, instead of them. You cooperate in their insanity and become a partner in perpetuating it and leaving it untreated. In that realm, you are truly abandoned in all senses of the word because you are left to be the crazy one and this is so isolating and deeply damaging.

The alternate choice is to believe that your caretakers are crazy. If you do, you live in a constant state of guardedness and fear because you recognize that crazy people cannot be trusted to care for themselves, or you, appropriately. If you are courageous enough to confront your caretakers and call them out on their insanity, you ensure that you will be ostracized from the family system and will take on the role of the outcast. Crazy people don't tend to admit that they are crazy.

As a child, neither of these options is safe. It is an impossible choice.

As I reflected on my own upbringing, I saw that initially I had chosen to believe that *I* was the crazy one. At some level I knew better because I did all sorts of things to help and save my parents from their own self-destruction. A great deal of my harmful focus remained, however, on me. My quest to be perfect was exhausting and painful. I thought that if only I could be better, smarter, prettier, more talented, funnier, and more loving I could change things. I thought that *I* held the key. I believed that *I* was the problem, because, again, I saw them as fine and me as damaged.

Over time, and perhaps by bringing myself to the brink of giving up completely on life, I attempted to change my perspective and got angry. I raged at my caretakers (which now included my step-father) and confronted them about their insanity and toxic behavior. My words were minimized and they teamed up, as unhealthy and addicted family systems do, and declared a war of sorts on me. They made me the "identified patient" and spoke of me like I was the damaged and crazy one.

It was so lonely. And so scary. Because, as a child (I was a teenager at the time), you feel ultimately powerless to change your situation. I was tempted to regress and go back to feeling like the crazy one because it was easier somehow. But you can't turn back the clock. So I stayed the course and the price I paid was losing my "hero" spot in the family. I was the "problem child" instead. Being the voice of reason did not win me any popularity contests, trust me.

Clearly, I needed a course on boundaries. It took me years, but I made it my personal mission to figure out the difference between <u>helping</u> people and feeling *responsible* for them. In order to not go certifiably crazy, I had to understand that other people's crises were not mine, unless I let them be. I came to understand the delicate difference between reacting and responding, which became so much easier the more psychological distance I achieved from those toxic people in my life.

When I could look at them like actors on a stage and not an extension of me, life got so much easier. You can deal with difficult people a whole lot easier when you see them as acting out their *own* life story, their *own* drama, and not as integral players in *yours*. You get to decide if you want to allow them to affect your mood: They aren't in charge of that. Do you want a part in their play? Do you want to offer them a starring role in yours? If not, just watch their performance and don't allow *their* "ick" to become *your* "ick." Instead, focus on surrounding yourself with positive people, people who make your life better for being in it. You're completely in control of that.

Example: Control What You Can. A delightful young woman I know has been struggling, like I did, with a father who just isn't stepping up to the plate to be a real "dad." She's wanted him to be a part of her life for years but he's totally checked out, not even calling or writing, let alone visiting with her. This makes her sad and anxious and she's torn up about it. She's written him letters and even requested to see him so that they can spend time together. She's becoming a young woman so fast and she wants her father not to miss out on her life. She wants his love and she wants to share hers with him. Unfortunately, this guy isn't the father she's hoped for. He's good for a minute and to make a promise, but then he backs out. He's a coward, bottom line. But she's young and hopeful and it's hard to face that. She imagines that it'll be different somehow, someday. And as unlikely as that is, she is stuck holding onto hope. To make things more complicated and painful, she remembers the bad times with him. She remembers his inappropriateness and her fear. But he's her dad and it's hard sometimes to let go of the hope that we have for someone and replace it with what the reality is.

So what can she do? She can focus on what she can control and leave the rest alone. She can't change him. She can't make him a better father. She can't convince him to be different. It's a romantic notion to think that she could, but she can't. Why? Because it's not her. She's not the reason he's not coming around. *He* is. *He's* the problem. *He's* the damaged and broken one. Being an adult doesn't make you mature. Being a father doesn't make you a dad. Whatever she thinks he should be doing, he isn't. She <u>has</u> to let go of what she thinks he "should" be doing because he's not affected by that. He's going to do whatever he's inclined to do, regardless of what she (or we) might think he should. She has the chance to be whole if she focuses on herself and what she's in charge of: Her own peace of mind. It's the very same as what you can control. Nothing more, nothing less. This is it. Your thoughts and interpretations. Your outward attitude. Your behaviors and actions. Your boundaries.

So why would you want to take this leap to stop trying to control things that are beyond yourself? To let go of the illusion that you can direct the Universe to fit your agenda? To focus on your own personal power, and nothing else? To take up all of the space in your own spirit and resist the impulse to step in and attempt to puppeteer someone else's life? Can you even imagine your life without that focus? A focus on the outside, on others and not on you. I challenge you to imagine it. It's a life of more peace and calm and less of one very destructive influence: Stress.

~Stress Less~

Somewhere along the way I heard a definition of stress that I've clung to ever since: Stress is caused by the difference between what we can control and what we can't. It's the gap that stresses us out.

Controllable Stuff − Uncontrollable Stuff = STRESS

The events are what the events are; it's how you relate to your perceived control over the situation that makes a difference to your mental and physical health. People are who they are: You can't control them, either.

Do you think you can control a great deal of events and people around you, yet despite your efforts, you can't seem to get a handle on it all and make things move in your targeted direction? Or, do you feel like you can't control anything and you're overwhelmed by the prospect that it's all out of your control?

Example: 30K Feet. I was flying recently and I heard a young man headed into what sounded like a full-on panic attack. He was shaking and crying, saying that we were all going to die when the plane crashed. He had all sorts of scenarios that he was playing out about how this was going to happen. I heard his mom ask him if there was anything he could do to change that? He said, "No, that's the problem!" She stayed calm and responded, "No, that's the solution. There is nothing you can do to change it. So, you have three choices: Fight it, trying to figure out a way to control something that you cannot control; accept it and be stressed out for the rest of the flight in fear that the worst is going to happen; accept it and let it go, knowing that whatever happens is out of your control so you may as well enjoy the flight."

I thought that was pretty sage advice, and although the child only calmed a little, the mom laid it out as best as she could. And she couldn't have been more right. Once you figure out that you cannot control something, the best way to reduce your stress is to accept that and focus only on the things that you can control. Accept the following statement as truth: You're along for the ride and you're not in the pilot's seat so consider getting into the plane, strapping in, following the safety instructions, leaving the flammables at home, and sitting back and enjoying the flight. Let the rest go.

~Let It Go~

"Anyone who has never made a mistake
has never tried anything new." ~ Albert Einstein

Maybe I need to say that again to you? Let the rest go. Let. It. Go. Holding onto the things you cannot control is like trying to fly a plane by hanging onto the wing. It cannot be done. And trying to <u>will</u> it to be done is going to blow your heart up like the Fourth of July. Literally. Do me a favor: Go watch a video on what happens to a heart under stress. It's frightening. Stress, in fact, does cause heart attacks. And a host of diseases. Do you want to cut your life short? If you think you'll live a long and healthy life in that state of stress, do you really *want* to?

Want less stress in your life? In order to have less stress, you have to reduce the gap between the things you're trying to control and those things you can actually control. And there is an inherent battle in that, and this fighting causes stress. If you want less stress you need to try to control fewer things. To make it easy, there are two types of control that I am encouraging you to let go of, whenever and however you can:

1. The control that stops you from asking for help ("Superhero Complex"), and,
2. The control that helps others from taking control that you want to hold onto ("Disposable Control").

~Superhero Complex~

I am stubborn. Okay, maybe that's an understatement, like saying a whale is big. I prefer to say that I'm "determined," but I keep getting corrected by those who know me best who say that I'm in a league of my own in the stubborn category. I like to think I'm getting better. There are certainly worse things I could be and this trait comes in handy. In keeping with my "determined" nature, when I set my mind to something, it's tough to remove me from that path. My former husband used to call me a "pit bull on a pork chop." Gives you quite the visual, doesn't it? Where does my stubbornness rears its ugliest head? Asking for help.

I used to have an anaphylactic reaction to reaching out to anyone for help. It was understandable since I felt that I owed my existence to my ability to "figure it out." The idea of handing over any control of that was frightening, to say the very least. Going through my divorce, and all of that stress, I realized that I wouldn't survive the process without some assistance and support. My friends have been conditioned over the years to assume that their offers of help will be rejected, so I have been amused at times to witness their reaction when I say "sure!" I have wondered if they may have wanted to retract their offers after the fact, never expecting my acceptance. Unfortunately, they are stuck with the "new and improved" me now!

Why does asking for help feel so uncomfortable? It means that you have a need, or needs, that you want met. If you are asking for help, at some level you are admitting that you might not be able to feed your needs without someone else stepping in. And what if they don't step in? What if they let you down? Not only do you have a need that hasn't been met but you also have disappointment in a relationship, in another person. You feel angry, annoyed, sad, or let down. Or maybe all of the above.

But, in the infamous words of Wayne Gretzky, "You miss 100% of the shots you don't take." Take a chance on the people in your world and see what happens. If they let you down by refusing your requests (yes, you need to give them more than one shot), you just got some information about your relationship. It's not necessarily damning data, but it tells you something. If you are always offering the help and not asking for it, it might just be that your circle of friends is caught off guard by this shift and they might need some time to adjust to the change.

Or, you may have surrounded yourself with takers and not givers, since you were filling the role of perpetual giver. Stepping out of that role is not easily done, for certain, but it allows for better balance in your relationships. And a lot less stress!

Exercise

Brainstorm your to-do list on the left side of a sheet of paper. On the right side, make a column entitled "resources." Under that heading, think about who might be able to help you complete that task. Maybe a friend who would like to spend some time with you and you could do so while you both pitch in on a project? Is there someone who is lonely who could use some company and might lend you a hand, with pleasure? Would Mom or Dad (or a sibling) help, maybe in trade? Write down some possibilities. Then tackle that list: Make a phone call, shoot a text, or send an email.

Being capable doesn't mean doing it all on your own. Adults ask (or should ask) for help, too, if they're smart. Be smart. *Ask*. Take off that superhero cape and allow someone to help you. And, in the process, know that you are helping them. You will feed your need for control by better addressing a shorter list of things to do, and you will feed their need for control by giving them something to be in charge of. It's a win-win. So what are you waiting for?

~Disposable Control~

You already know (I hope) that you cannot control everything, everywhere, and at every point in time. There are certain things that you want to make sure that you control ("do or die" elements). But are there things that you can give up control over in order to make an experience and/or a relationship better? These things fall under the category of "disposable control." When you run into a person who is trying to control a situation or things in it, put them in charge of something so that they don't take it from you where it counts. Give them something to control intentionally: Feed their need for control. If you don't want them poking their nose into project A, assign them project B.

A few years back, I was on a field trip and one of the kids was acting up, wanting to be in charge of where he went and what we were doing at any given moment. The teacher, a seasoned veteran, made the child the "Official Water Bottle Holder" for her. Like a light switch, that boy's attitude went from troublemaker to line leader in a flash. He stood taller, smiled, and walked with purpose. He was large and in charge: Of a water bottle, just a water bottle. But he was "in charge" now and that fed his need for control. The teacher was certainly quite capable of carrying her own water bottle, but she pretended (for the sake of peace and harmony) to need to have her water bottle carried by a "capable" person. It worked, and everyone on the trip benefitted.

You can do the very same thing in your world by assigning control to someone instead of wrestling with them for it. If you're working on a group project, for instance, and you're in charge of a part of the write up and another member is stepping on your toes, find a juicy part to put them in charge of. It's incredibly productive and a whole lot less exhausting than what you're doing now, I assure you. Identify an area of disposable control and toss it to someone and watch what happens when you feed that need. It will be noteworthy.

~Think You Can Control Your Image? ~

The answer is a little bit "yes" and a little bit "no." People believe what they want to about you. You cannot make them like you or see you for who you really are if they don't want to. I used to be "that girl" who thought that I was a horrible person if *everyone* didn't like me. If *anyone* could think of a reason to dislike me then I *had* to fix it. Woman, *please*. Trust me, it's a trap to spend all sorts of energy trying to control your image and make sure it's exactly what you want it to be so that others will think a certain thing about you. Because, by definition, an image is not real: It leads people to believe things that may or may not be true about you.

It's a delicate balancing act between truth and fiction when we attempt to control the image we project to the outside world. Making sure we look good, smile appropriately, dress the part, and so on are good things to do because they help to show on the outside what we feel on the inside and to get for us the things we think that we deserve in life. The danger comes when what we are putting on the outside is not a reflection of what we feel or believe on the inside. When we compromise who we really are for external acceptance, we lose ourselves. In our teen years (and well beyond, trust me), we place a great deal of importance on image. Unfortunately, it's not time or energy well spent.

Example. Imposter Syndrome. When I was a teenager (during the time right after dinosaurs left, to hear my eldest daughter tell it), I had <u>all sorts</u> of control issues. And when I say "all sorts" I mean I was steps away from going batshit crazy if I couldn't be in charge of certain things. The problem was that I was in control of nothing really. My family was addicted and struggling with lots of mental illness (and abuse and so on and so on) so I certainly wasn't in any sort of control there. My father came in and out of my life like a girl changes her underwear so I was practically in crisis on the daily when it came to being able to anticipate "what next" with Daddy-O.

So, what did I do to survive? I focused on controlling my image. I tried on every eating disorder on the menu, sometimes bulimic, sometimes anorectic, sometimes a compulsive overeater. I paid attention in school and got good grades (well, better than a number of my friends) so I could be the "smarty pants." I was perky and cheery and helped everyone I could.

What did this all get me? I never felt real. I never felt calm. I never felt like *me*. I felt like an imposter all the time, trying super hard to be cheerful and pretty and smart and all the while I felt sad and ugly and stupid. My friend, Gail, called me "fake" and she wasn't so wrong. I *was* fake. I wasn't on the inside who I tried to present to the world on the outside. I was afraid to feel how sad I was, let alone let anyone else see it. If I couldn't be pretty and thin I couldn't imagine surviving. For all intents and purposes, I was slowly killing myself but I didn't seem to care. The mask I was wearing was too important to release.

What changed? I hit rock bottom and had to crawl my way back up. And it was no fun. I don't remember my high school years with a great deal of fondness. Instead, those years have a cloud over them because Bridget wasn't really there. Who she pretended to be and who she was trying hard to be was there, but not the real, flawed, hurting Bridget who was struggling underneath. Like a vampire, she hid from the light.

As I made my way through college I had to face my demons and wrestle with who I really was, flaws and all. It took years to get to a better place with myself and to let go of the need to be perfect (or at least my version of it). I came to understand that the only thing I can control is *my* end of things. Take a look at models and actresses who are known for their beauty. Then read a few celebrity newspapers or tweets and you'll see that even the most gorgeous people get criticized for some imperfection. Perfection is an illusion, and you cannot control what other people think of your crafted image. They are going to see what they are going to see and there isn't a darn thing you can do about it. So, let it go. For your health and your sanity.

One of the most troubling observations I've made in my work is the sheer number of people who are going through life without letting the world know who they really are. They are trapped behind masks that build walls between them and other people, often unconsciously. As long as the image remains intact, everything is considered to be "fine." You're fitting in with your group of friends? Great. Nothing else matters.

Wrong. You matter. Peer pressure to fit it can be no big deal if it makes you a better person: If fitting in means that you bathe and groom yourself and do well in school and are working hard at your sport or other extracurricular.

On the other hand, if fitting in means that you are expected to dress and behave in a certain way than who you really are, then it's a problem. Peer pressure is just a term usually reserved for teens that is called "group norms" in the big, bad adult world. Yes, we have them, too. A lot of communities are a lot like high school in that you're expected to wear the right clothes, drive the right cars, live in the right neighborhood, and so on. And plenty of adults sacrifice their sanity just to fit in through overworking, overspending, or just obsessing about how they are perceived by others.

Can I tell you a secret? Anyone worth having in your life won't leave if you fly your freak flag high and become who you really are. Sure, you might not be homecoming king or queen but if that's not who you think it's important to be, why do you care?

I know it's easier in some ways to suck it up and fit in no matter what, but I suspect that quite a number of you reading this book know that "fitting in" can also have grave consequences when it starts to involve alcohol, drugs, sex, and other risk-taking behaviors. And then there's depression and anxiety that is multiplied by the stress of fitting in. That has a whole other set of risk factors. Still want to sell out?

If so, I suspect you've signed on to a set of rules and expectations that are not letting the real "you" out. They are keeping you cloaked. Billy Joel called it "the stranger." (If you don't know the song reference, look it up; it's old school but it's worth a listen). It's the person within the person, the one behind the mask. The "true you" who has been forgotten about. It's like when we get everybody all dolled up for the Christmas photo. We don't really look like that, but, boy, are we photogenic?! Are you in your Christmas best around the clock? Do you even remember who you are without the mask?

See, if you think about it, you can never escape yourself. You are the product of your biology *and* your experiences. You are a product of your culture and your relationships. You are also a product of your beliefs, attitudes, and thoughts. Most of all, you are a product of your choices.

You can choose to fill out the space in your own skin, or reduce yourself into a smaller, less-real version of yourself. You can succumb to peer pressure or you can be who you really are and be proud of it. That's a choice. It's a choice you make every day whether you do it consciously or not. Most of the choices we make are subconscious. Like breathing. We are on auto-pilot with our behavior much of the time and we tend to just float through life without considering the fact that we can choose something else for ourselves. But we can.

~Influence Others~

If you're honest with yourself, you'll find that the idea of being in control of other people has great appeal. Does that sound offensive to you? Well, it's true for 99.9% of us, more so than we are willing to take ownership of. Think on that for a minute: What if you could get that annoying friend to stop creating distraction and drama (or pick annoyance of your choice and insert here)? You'd jump on that like a moth to a flame. We would love to be in control of other people, some more than others and at some times more than others. Yet, saying, "I'm a controlling person" is socially unacceptable so we attempt to hide that trait like covering up a pimple before prom. It's still there, folks.

Control, and our efforts to control things and people, is not bad in and of itself. As you read earlier, having or seeking no control is ripe with problems. And the same can be said for having too much. It's a balancing act between controlling what we can and should and letting go of the rest. And you have to start with you: Focus your efforts inward and being in charge of what *you* think, feel, believe, and do. And then set that example with those around you. As a result, you won't be "controlling" them, but you will influence them greatly and that is powerful.

So, you can't control others, but you *can* influence them. How? In pretty much the same way that they influence you. Through your attitude, your actions, and your boundaries. What you do affects what others do. When I'm in a good mood and doing fun things with others, it's contagious. When I'm cranky, same thing goes. So how can you influence others in a positive way? The concept of MSR (Model It, Seek It, Reward It) offers a way to help others get their needs met, as well as a way to role model all sorts of other healthy, effective attitudes and behaviors. It's a simple, intuitive three-step process.

Model It. The buck starts and stops with you, so be what you want others to be. And not just when it's easy. You have to be consistent through good times and bad. It's not enough to *say* that you value certain behaviors; you have to *show* that you do. If you want to know what others really value, don't listen to what they say. Observe what they spend their time and their money on.

Seek It. Be active in looking for other people doing what you want them to do. Don't just sit back and wait to see some miraculous change: Be on constant watch for it. Ask about it. Start conversations. Be an active voice in the change process.

Reward It. When you see others demonstrating those positive behaviors, reward them. Pay them a compliment. Give them something that means something to them. Spend some time with them. Smile.

The bottom line is you can influence others, but at the end of the day, people will do what they want to do. You can put out an invitation, make the food, set the table, and decorate your house, but you can't make people come to your party and eat your cake.

~*Claim Your Stoke*~

Ready to focus on being comfortable with yourself and your choices by turning down the volume of the other voices you've been listening to? You need to start living intentionally and be in charge of your own destiny. Since you haven't done it before so it might feel new and strange. And you may be intimidated. That's totally normal. Don't worry: The Universe will conspire to guide you. It'll throw opportunity after opportunity in your path so that you can live differently. And those opportunities may look like challenges or problems, but rest assured that they are there to invite you to break out of your comfort zone. To try on your new identity. Know that if you don't grab those chances when they first appear, bigger and more dramatic options will follow. It's sort of like when your mom texts you to check in and you don't respond right away: Watch out because she WILL track you down. The Universe is just as annoying and a *lot* more creative.

And if you ignore later chances, watch yourself, because it may feel like you're hovering over the edge of a cliff, dangling by a thread, hoping to grab ahold of something, anything. It's like the guy who is in a massive flood. As the water is building up in the streets, someone pulls up in a truck and offers him a ride out to safety. The guy says, "No, thank you. I'm waiting for God to save me." A short time later, the water is now flooding his house. A boat pulls up and asks if he wants a ride. He refuses, citing God's impending arrival again. Not long after, the man is now perched on his roof with water cresting at the roofline. A helicopter throws him a line and the man refuses it, saying, "God will save me." The man eventually drowns sitting there on his rooftop and he proceeds up to Heaven. The man is crazily mad at God, saying, "Why didn't you save me?" God replies, "I sent you a truck, a boat, and a helicopter. What were you waiting for?"

Don't wait for things to be perfect: They won't ever be perfect for more than a moment. And don't beat yourself up trying to make everything perfect. Perfection is an illusion. Control what you can, feel that need fed, and move forward.

Seek to demonstrate your "power" through influence (versus control) and you will make your world better, and that will, by definition, make the world a better place. And if you're still stuck on thinking that in order to have a good life you have to control every last detail, or ELSE, I leave you with this quote:

> *"Don't take life too seriously. No one gets out alive."*
> ~ *Cocktail Napkin*

Control

~End of Chapter Inventory~

"The question isn't who is going to let me;
it's who is going to stop me." ~ Ayn Rand

Summary: Control is a deep-seated human need. Finding a balance between influence and control is necessary to foster positive relationships and support success.

Key Concepts:

- Control pops up highest when fear is high and trust in low in relationships.
- You can control your thoughts, interpretations, behaviors, actions, attitude, and boundaries.
- Boundaries are essential in navigating control.
- You can influence others, but you cannot control them.

What are three takeaways you have from this chapter? What did you learn about yourself and/or others? What shifts in thinking did you experience as a result of reading this chapter?

Takeaway 1:

Takeaway 2:

Takeaway 3:

Rate yourself on your confidence and competence practicing the key concepts in this chapter:

1: I'm so lousy I don't want to respond

2

3

4

5: I'm okay, but I have a lot to learn

6

7

8

9

10: I'm going to write my own book on this competency

What are three things you commit to do (differently) as a result of reading this chapter? Think of things that will improve your life personally, spiritually, emotionally, and physically.

Commitment 1:

Commitment 2:

Commitment 3:

What are three roadblocks/challenges to being where you need to be? What are three things (relationships, habits, assumptions, situations) that you need to adjust and/or remove in order to live happier?

Roadblock 1:

Roadblock 2:

Roadblock 3:

What are three strategies for addressing those roadblocks and challenges? What are three changes you could make that would reduce or remove the obstacles you have?

Strategy 1:

Strategy 2:

Strategy 3:

"If you aim at nothing,
you'll hit it every time." ~ B.J. Marshall

6

VALIDATION

"Put yourself in a state of mind where you say to yourself, 'Here is an opportunity for me to celebrate like never before, my own power, my own ability to get myself to do whatever is necessary.'"
~ Martin Luther King, Jr.

Trees grow toward the sun. Seems simple enough to understand. They seek the light and they find it or they die. And they will grow in unbelievable ways to get to the light. Sideways. L-shaped. Seemingly so tilted that you'd think that they'd fall over. This has always fascinated me.

I have a tree in the woods right behind my house that looks like a bendy straw: It shifts from side to side throughout its midsection. The trees are dense back there but they've thinned out over the years, so the trees that were surrounding this tree have mostly disappeared. This crazy tree must have had to grow in and around its neighbors in order to secure sunlight. But it prevailed. Its struggle did not mean its demise. It kept seeking the sun, and kept finding it. And it kept growing.

The tree is just like you and me. We seek the light to nourish us and help us to grow. But our light is not the physical sun: It's another building block. It's having the light shine on us, to illuminate us, to show others who we are. It's validation. Being cared about and valued.

Noticed. Acknowledged for what we bring to the table. Understood. Appreciated.

What does it mean to be validated? The dictionary definition is "to recognize, establish, or illustrate the worthiness or legitimacy of" (Merriam-Webster.com). When someone validates your experience they might do it with compassion ("that must feel terribly") or joint anger ("I can't believe they did that to you!"). In some cases, it's in a knowing look, touch, or the comfort that comes from a calm presence in the face of a storm. It's that "OMG!" text you get when you're shared some big news. It's that friend that comes to sit with you and just be with you as you cry. She's telling you that she "gets" you and that you're not alone or crazy. Well, maybe a little crazy, but the cute kind of crazy. That you're understood, and maybe you're in a bad situation, but that doesn't make you bad.

You might be one of those people who says that you don't do the things you do for the attention you attract. You say that you don't need validation. Validation is for insecure, needy people. You're no attention whore. You're elevated. Self-actualized. I might buy that if you can admit that doing the things that you do makes you feel good on the inside, and that's all you seek. Intrinsic reward. You don't want to have the masses to fall at your feet in appreciation. Instead, you take care of yourself. Either way, I hate to tell you this, you superhero you, but you have an innate need to feel validated. Whether it's from you or from others, even the rock stars among us *need* validation. Whoa, yeah, especially the attention-seeking rock stars! Just ask their managers and publicists...

~Nice Guy/Girl Syndrome~

In order to meet your need for validation, you might do a whole host of things. Usually the things you do to feel validated from others are positive (performing kind acts, accomplishing your goals, keeping yourself healthy and attractive). "Positive" can be hijacked, however. It can be morphed into something negative and destructive if taken to the extreme. "How" you ask?

Take "performing kind acts" as an example. Generosity is a wonderful thing and we are called to help one another out, to make the journey of life a little easier. But what happens when you overextend yourself? Focus on taking care of others, excluding your needs? Not only will you suffer burnout at some point, but resentment will set in. There are an endless supply of people who do things for others with the (hidden) expectation that those people will "owe" them at some point down the line. I know I've found myself in the position of turning myself inside out for a friend only to find that they couldn't be bothered to offer anything that I needed when it was my "turn." There I was, on my proverbial knees, and you could have heard a cricket chirp. Nothing. No offer of help. Nada. Silence. And that hurt. Deeply.

Pain offers to teach us something if we pay attention, so I took this hurtful moment to ask myself about my "giving" nature. I was uncomfortable when I recognized that giving to others wasn't all altruistic for me. I was getting something out of it more than a warm, fuzzy feeling. It was my way of connecting to other people and endearing myself to them. My childhood built a wild fear of abandonment in me, and although I've worked for years to loosen its hold on my psyche, it holds on hard and pops up when I least expect it. Although I can't quote it directly, I'm pretty certain that my subconscious was saying something like, "hey, if I'm nice and giving and help my friends in all these ways, they'll want to keep me around cuz they'll need me and when you need someone you don't leave them." Sigh. It doesn't work that way, fortunately and unfortunately. People will find a way to get their needs met so if they don't want to need you, they won't. They'll leave you, and all your "giving" won't matter worth a scratch. They may be indebted to you, but it may be a debt they'll never repay.

And if they stick around, you may grow to hate the dance you've choreographed. You have needs, too. Needs that ache to be filled no matter how "generous" or "self-sufficient" you are. Having it all together isn't a bad thing, but if you have a hidden agenda (having your actions reciprocated or acknowledged), you may be disappointed. Disappointment, unchecked and unresolved, breeds resentment. It may be subtle at first ("why don't they appreciate all that I do for them?" "why don't they acknowledge my giving ways?"), but it will grow. You can only deny meeting your own needs for so long. Others are not likely to be appreciative enough to make up for us being so self-sacrificing. When resentment takes hold, it spreads like a cancer and destroys everything in its path. There is another way.

~Feel Validated~

If that section above sounds familiar, the question is how can you meet your need to be validated without going overboard and drowning in the process? Just like anything, it's about moderation. Have you ever gone to a party and eaten way too much? You're literally about to pop the button on your pants you're so full. Maybe you even unbuttoned your pants and pulled your shirt down lower so you could breathe. Or wore leggings or sweats to begin with. The food tasted good going down, for sure, but now you're way beyond full. And being that full doesn't feel good. It feels constricting and sickening.

Close your eyes and go to a time when you felt like that. Experience the discomfort. Feel the ick factor of going too far with a good thing. It works the very same way with "nice." There can be too much "nice." Only instead of fullness and bloating, your body feels exhaustion, stress, and resentment. If you ate just enough, you'd feel full. Your hunger would be satisfied. When you're "nice" you can feed your need for validation by giving "just enough" of yourself, and no more.

When you've given more than you should, no amount of validation will take care of you. You've martyred yourself for others and your resources are depleted. Plus, people can't possibly thank you enough for what you do for them when you're running on empty. And guess what? You're really not doing them any favors.

Think back: Have you ever been the recipient of a martyr's "gifts?" At first you might be thankful for what they give to you. After a while, though, you just feel guilty. They won't do anything for themselves. They just give, give, give. If you ask them what you can do for them, the response is always the same, "Oh, nothing. I'm fine."

But they are not fine. They are so focused on the outside and showing their concern for others that they forget to take care of themselves. They forget to nurture and thank themselves for all that they do. What do we often do when we want to thank someone for something they've done for us? We give them a "thank you" gift.

What would the world be like if when we did something nice for someone else in turn we did something nice for ourselves? What if we validated ourselves? Do you think that there would be less dysfunction and conflict in relationships? I'll bet that we would feel less disappointed, focus more on the giving, and feel more satisfied in our relationships. There would be fewer hidden agendas, less martyrdom, and more celebrating.

They say "charity starts at home." Can we agree to start validation there, too? To not only acknowledge others for what they do for us, but appreciate ourselves when we do a good thing? What would that feel like? Wouldn't you agree that we'd be even more grateful and joyous the more we fed this need in ourselves and others?

Exercise

Draft and send yourself a thank you note. Mail it to yourself. Yes, you're worth a stamp. No, you can't just put it in your own mailbox. Go to the trouble of addressing it and stamping it. And no, you can't text it to yourself. The only thing I might not recommend is to put it in your mailbox, stamped. Your postal carrier may not have read this book carefully and might, well, scratch his head trying to figure out what you're up to. My mailman wouldn't blink an eye if I did that since he knows me well. But unless you live in my neighborhood, play it safe and actually go to the post office or visit one of those big blue bins and drop it in. Again, you're worth it. And just think of the chuckle you'll have when you receive it in your mailbox. It really is the little things in life that make all the difference.

~Insecurity & The Drama Dance~

Do you have a friend who seems to always have a crisis that needs fixing? If there was a magnet that attracted drama, she'd be holding onto it tightly, almost hungering for the next "crazy" thing that she needs help to address. Now, I'm not talking about the "bad things that happen to good people" person, who just seems to just attract more than her fair share of mayhem. No, I'm talking about the friend who continually and repeatedly drives to the edge of the cliff and wonders why she's feeling overwhelmed and anxious and why she has more problems than she has resources.

What's at the core of this pattern? Often times, it's addiction and/or mental illness, plain and simple. And I don't mean necessarily something that can be easily diagnosed or medicated. It's illness of the mind, and heart. If it doesn't rise to the level of a diagnosis and prescribed meds, it's clearly unhealthy and it roots from a number of sources, mostly a need for validation of their pain. Whether they will admit it or not, they want validation for being the victim in their own melodrama. "Oh, you poor thing!" Acting upon the world is too scary so they see fit to be acted upon and to create or co-create situations where people can rescue them or at the very least commiserate with them. Bottom line: This is the need for validation gone tragically wrong. Instead of being okay with simply being seen by others, they are addicted to being SEEN (in all caps, bright lights, with a loud soundtrack playing in the background) by others.

And what's it like being a relationship with a drama whore? Exhausting. At first you might not even notice that you've been sucked into a drama vortex. You might just be so focused on offering empathy and understanding and support (all components of validation) that you don't notice that they are sucking your very life force from you. They are constantly needing you to rescue them from their latest disaster and as frustrating as this may be, you find yourself running to snatch them from the jaws of destruction before you examine your role in their unending drama. Because you do have a role. If you are validating them and rescuing them you are colluding with them in their drama dance. You're giving their drama air time. And just like Pavlov's dogs (if you don't know this psychological experiment, look it up; the reference comes in handy and will make you look wicked smart), they respond to your attention by seeking more of it. And no matter what you give, it's never enough. They need more attention than anyone can provide. They aren't satisfied, ever. They have a tank that can't be filled. They are battling with profound insecurity and are filling it with validation for their drama, not who they are. It's like being popular because of the clothes you wear and not the person you are (sound familiar?). You're getting attention for the wrong reasons which leaves you feeling empty and unfulfilled. Your need for validation isn't being met. Right arrow, wrong target.

~Stop the MADNESS!~

Okay, adrenaline junkie, knock it off. Stop. Or at a minimum, slow the heck down. Don't race to their side as soon as the next drama is reported. Breathe. Wait. Hesitate. And when you do respond, be calmer than you've been. Don't "oooh" and "aaah" and match their emotion. Be calm. Ask questions like, "did you see that coming?" Or, "what could you have done to avoid this?" Or just say as close to nothing as you can. It's like oxygen and fire: Being emotional and giving your friend attention for the behavior feeds it and makes it stronger.

That goes for you, too. If you're a drama seeker and you find yourself texting your list of friends to share your latest and greatest "oh, no!" moment, stop. Pause. Ask yourself if you can handle this one on your own, quietly and without fanfare. Take an honest examination of how you got there. Ask yourself some hard-hitting questions. What could you have done to prevent (or lessen) this situation? If you flunk a class, it's not a last minute crisis. You've known your grades on your assignments all semester and year. You didn't do your homework or study for your tests. This is no surprise. This happens in people's lives, but it doesn't make it a crisis. It makes it a problem, one that you can plan for better than you did. Learn from it. Don't keep recreating it. And take inventory of the "high" you're getting from getting so close to the cliff's edge and not falling over it.

If you're like me, and grew up in an addicted family system, you may be drawn to be an adrenalin junkie. You may seek situations where you can feel anxiety so you can feel alive. Does danger excite you? I'm not talking about rollercoasters. I'm talking about setting your life on fire and then trying to rescue it out of the flames. It's not healthy. It wreaks havoc on your immune system. It's a form of addiction. It's time for you to visit a 12-Step meeting. Or go talk with a therapist. I mean it. Go. Before you can't rescue yourself effectively. Life doesn't have to be like that. You can be validated for simply being you, not being the victim in your own story.

~*Suffering Mindset*~

The late, great psychiatrist Sigmund Freud contended that people have two drives: The pursuit of pleasure and the avoidance of pain. I've studied people all of my life and I studied Freud in undergrad and graduate school and something about it just didn't jive with my experiences and observations. I know a countless number of people who seem to constantly go after things that cause them pain. Bad relationships, unsatisfying jobs, unhealthly habits, and so on. So what gives? Was Freud wrong?

Not necessarily. I think it comes down to one thing: For some, pain is pleasure. And I'm not talking about a "50 Shades of Gray" scenario. There are countless people out there who feel deserving of pain at some level, so pain is desired, and therefore, pleasurable. Or, and related to this, pain makes them feel alive. You could be going through your daily routine in a drone-like state, only to hit up against sharp corner, stubbing your pinkie toe something fierce. You're awake now! Psychologically I've seen the same thing hold true for people: They don't feel sufficiently "awake" without pain. And what is one of the big magnets for creating painful experiences in our lives and having a suffering mindset? Focusing on the pain by complaining incessantly about it.

I could write an entire book about complaining: The tendency we have to engage in it, its ill effects, and how it bonds us to one another. Try this: The next time you're in a group, share a complaint about something common to everyone. The weather should work if it's rained or been slightly chilly or moderately hot. Then track the responses you get. I guarantee you that nearly everyone will say something to commiserate with you. And we love it. We seek it. We need it.

But, wait! We were talking about validation and gratitude and all that feel good stuff just a second ago. Isn't that the opposite of complaining? It is, yet, complaining is the glue that connects us to one another, the common thread that links us in our human condition. And in our misery, we seek company. Not just for the connection (as you've read about earlier in this book), but also for the validation of our pain. We want our pain to be appreciated. We want recognition for the path we've walked. We want to be seen for our ability to withstand pain and challenge. For our frizzy hair because we had to walk a block in the rain. For our bad mood because our parents treat each other like garbage. For our bad grades because we struggle with a learning disability. For the extra weight we carry because food comforts us. We want others to feel for us when the going is tough.

~*What's Tough…and Enough?*~

I was visiting a friend recently and I made some teriyaki steak and chicken for dinner. Admittedly, I'm not the world's best cook. I'm not the world's worst cook, mostly because I know that there are some cooks out there who could be arrested for abuse for serving their cooking to human beings. Anyway, I didn't have the best cut of steak, and while slicing it into strips, I sliced my finger. Have I mentioned that I'm a klutz? And I was cooking on an electric stovetop and outdoor electric grill, two things I never use. Are you sensing the foreboding yet?

I think you may have already figured out that I totally messed up the meal, especially the steak. And with a vengeance. It was the hardest, driest, blandest steak I think I've ever cooked. And that is saying a *lot*. As I served it to my daughters and friend I apologized and admitted that it was tough and dry and I wouldn't be offended if no one ate it. Having grown up poor, my friend rarely had steak as a kid. For those of you who are unaware, steak is pretty expensive. And those of us who grew up poor, having fresh meat for dinner was a luxury. So, he shared a story from his childhood when a similar thing happened when his grandmother made a steak dinner. Her husband (his grandfather) complained when he bit into the steak that it was tough. She replied, "It'd be tougher if you didn't have any steak." Go, Grandma!

Are you grateful for the steak or focused on how it doesn't live up to your expectations? Do you thank your lucky stars for the roof over your head, or complain about your room isn't big or cool enough? Do you open the fridge and smile, seeing how much food you have in there, or slam the door because you don't have your favorite food? We live in an entitled and materialistic society but we can either buy into that and take things for granted, or blaze our own path and be grateful for every little thing we are blessed to receive. It's much more fun that way.

I remember when I was in kindergarten, my best friend's mom used to tell us that we needed to finish the food on our plates because people in Africa were starving and would be grateful for our scraps. Kerry and I contemplated how we could wrap and ship our leftovers to these poor people in Africa. Her mom chuckled at us when we suggested that, though I think she really thought that we were being fresh. We were only six years old and already we were battling with how to show our gratefulness properly. Wanting to be finished when we were full, yet feeling like we were ungrateful if we stopped.

Which begs the question: Can you be grateful and at the same time still want for more? Does wanting things you don't have make you ungrateful for the things you already possess? The two conditions (gratitude and desire) can, indeed, co-exist. You can be having an amazing steak and potatoes dinner and still want a big slice of that key lime pie for dessert. The balancing act is being grateful despite wanting more. Can you enjoy what you have even though you may want more?

~Come From Gratitude~

Want less drama and heartache? Start with being grateful for what you do have and use less energy trying to acquire what you don't have. You attract what you focus on, so if you're looking for drama, you're sure to find it. If you're looking for what's bad in the world, I can offer at least fifteen 24-hour "news" stations devoted to showing you.

What if you looked instead for the good stuff? What if you started thinking about what you're grateful for more than what you're mad or sad about? That's a real game changer, provided you've bought into the laws of attraction. So what is it that makes a person innately grateful? I've pondered this question a great deal as the years have passed and I've stumbled down this bumpy road of life. It seems like just yesterday that I was a teenager, twisted in my own grief and anger and fear and disappointment with my family and their splintered lives. I am quite certain that from where they stood, I was an ungrateful and problematic noise that they wished that they could hit the "mute" button for.

As a mother myself now, one of my big triggers is when my children behave in an entitled way. Like no matter what wonderful things they just received, if there was just a hair out of place, it made the whole experience an exercise in torture for them. I joked with one of my daughters recently that I was willing to bet if she won a million dollars she'd focus on how unfair it was that she had to pay taxes with half of it. It wouldn't make her giddy with excitement and unending gratitude that she was a *half* a million dollars richer. Nope. She'd be bitching about the unfairness of high taxes and what she could have done with the other half a million bucks.

Sound familiar? Be honest. When you're asked if you're a glass half-empty or half-full sort of person, do you automatically say "half full" because it's the popular response? Who wants to be known as the Eeyore among us? Okay, a few. My stepfather, for example, was so grumpy that he insisted on being called "Grumpa." If the shoe fits....

Aside from the health benefits of being an optimist (and therefore the health costs of being a pessimist), do you think you'd have a life with more fun and joy if you were optimistic? I know, I know; being a pessimist is in vogue when you're a teenager. So, for those of you pessimists out there, I can just hear you now giving me a short list of reasons as to how that rhetorical question wasn't so rhetorical. It might go something like, "pessimists are right more often and therefore disappointed less." Okay. You've got me there. You may be right on that one. But life is a whole lot more enjoyable when you're not focused on the ick and the suck and the messy that life can be. And I know that teens are excused for being moody and cranky, but the hormones and changes only account for so much; you've more in charge of your attitude that you might be letting on. I challenge you to give turning it around a real chance.

While I was drafting this book, I bumped into a guy while I was out running errands. We were both smiling about the warm, sunny weather we were having. I could tell quickly that he liked being happy as much as I did so I told him about the books I was writing and how it's much more socially acceptable to be unhappy than happy. He said, "I know. Why are so many people going through life miserable? I woke up this morning and was happy that I got another day!"

Is that how you feel? Do you get up in the morning and appreciate the gift of another sunrise? Not so much? What would happen if you said, "THANK YOU!" as you opened your eyes in the morning? I predict very good things. Give it a whirl tomorrow morning, being careful to not to scare your family by being TOO loud. You might totally freak them out. Ease into the out loud happy if your family members have nervous dispositions or are Eeyores themselves. For now, just say it in your head, with a smile on your face. See what happens to the rest of your day.

To do this doesn't mean that you have to be in La La Land and think that unicorns dance in rainbows and vrap Skittles. It's just where you place your primary focus. Is it on what there is to be thankful for or what there is to be annoyed by? Where is your sight set? It's like taking a photo of someone's house: You can point the lens toward the house, angling down the side where the colorful flower garden is, or you can shoot the garbage cans on the other side. It's still the same house. Just a different focal point. That's life. There are plenty of garbage cans. And plenty of flower gardens. Which would you rather look at? The choice is yours.

~*Gratitude Practices*~

If you believe in manifestation (bringing what you want to have into your life by thinking good thoughts about it and believing it to be on its way to you), you'll immediately see the connection between being grateful and being abundant: If you are grateful for what you have, you will attract more of it. So create a gratitude journal to record those thoughts. Every single client of mine who has started a gratitude journal into their routine has reaped astounding results. Make it a practice to write in your gratitude journal on a daily basis. Here are some suggestions for incorporating gratitude (including, but not limited to, a journal) into your life:

- Write down three things that you're grateful for;
- Journal about one positive experience you had;
- Send a text or email to someone, thanking or complimenting them on something they did;
- Meditate for a few minutes on images of all the things you're grateful for;

- Commit a "random act of kindness" and write about it;
- Make a "gratitude collage," with images of the things you're grateful for and post it on your bathroom, bedroom, or closet door so you can see it every day.

If you don't yet believe in manifestation, a gratitude journal still works. How? If you focus on good things, you notice more good things. *Whatever it is that you focus on, you have more of it.*

My grandfather had the corner on this insight. If I ever complained about a body ache or pain, he'd say, "Why don't I cut off your arm?" The first time I heard this I was horrified: Whose grandfather says THAT? But he added the key statement to that: "Then you'll forget all about your sore ankle." He understood at a core level that whatever you focus your attention on *owns* you. If you want get your focus onto something else, you can choose a new focal point, or let the world do it for you.

The pivotal point rests on the choice: It's all yours. You get to choose where you focus; what you give your attention and energy to. Why not make it something positive? They say that pessimists are right more often, but they are unhappier, sicker, and die earlier. Grateful people are optimistic. Not self-deluding, but optimistic. After you focus on the things in your life to be grateful for you find more and more things to be grateful for and you start to expect things to happen in your life that are good. Even things that might be viewed as neutral show their sunny side. And you find the silver linings in the bad stuff.

You *create* in your world what you *expect* in your world. Read that sentence again. No, one more time. Can you hear that? That what you have today is based on the choices you've made in the past? The choices you've made in the past were based on what you expected to have. And now you have what you've expected. Are you selling yourself short? Are you suffering to punish yourself (or someone else) for some sin or wrongdoing in the past? If you expect good, you'll create opportunities to have good in your life. And it works beautifully. In the opposite direction, too. And don't be mistaken: *Hope* and *expectation* are very different. You can hope your life away, while still expecting bad fortune. Expecting good things can and will transform your existence.

~Yay, Me!~

You might not do it publicly, but when you've made it to the other side of something challenging you're apt to give yourself a little pat on the back. "Good job, Me. I rock." You don't? Okay, then you really need to work on that. Life shows us so many twists and turns and we have to navigate our way. When we don't run off the road and crash we deserve kudos.

When we don't acknowledge ourselves for overcoming something yucky, we miss out. We also show loyalty to the yuck. We send a message that we want more of it. "Once wasn't enough, send me more!" When is enough, enough? When will you be done holding on to the things that don't serve you and make you feel badly about the world. Can't you celebrate what you have? Would that be so terrible?

Want to feel more satisfied right away? Want to feel your needs getting met in the next five minutes? Stop the suffering mindset. It's ok to love school. It's wonderful to love your family. Your friends. Your house. Your body. People will be jealous. Instead of apologizing or justifying the happy you have say, "Isn't it AWESOME? My life is so great!!" You don't have to brag; just focus on the good stuff.

One of my favorite clients, an entrepreneur of inspirational proportions and kid at heart, used to uplift me with his responses and demeanor about his work. When I would ask him how he was doing or how work was going, he would always respond with "Awesome (or fabulous, or terrific), Doc (his nickname for me)!" And he meant it. With every fiber of his being he meant it. He felt fabulous. He felt motivated. He felt on top of the world. Was his business the best it could be? No. But it was moving forward and he got to do just what he wanted to do and that was bliss. Being himself and being successful at the same time: It was awesome.

Life is too short to be helpless. You can be a tremendous victim, but why? Where does that get you? As you read about in the chapter on control, claim what's yours and drive it. That's what life is all about. It's not about waiting for the next bad thing to happen so you can add a paragraph to your sob story. It's not a pity fest. For some, but not for you.

You're reading this book for a reason, so be grateful for that. Be grateful that you've found your way to this paragraph and drop the victim stance. If you've been victimized, you have my deep support and compassion, and I want you to seek support to find ways to deal with those experiences in a way that doesn't cost you any more of your happiness. If you're not really a victim, please save feeling like a victim for when you really are one. I can tell you that being a true victim is rare. As you learned in the control chapter, you always have influence. And your influence in the gratitude arena is to focus on what's right and start there.

~Validating the Blessing of Struggle~

"It's okay not to be okay.
Sometimes it's hard to follow your heart" ~ Jessie J.

Pain is such a great motivator. And suppressant. Sometimes when I'm in pain, I want to act, to move, to go, and to get as far away from that feeling as I possibly can. I start projects, I volunteer for things, I offer to counsel friends, run errands, and the list keeps growing. I used to paint a room every time one of my lovers hurt me. He may not have loved me, but Benjamin Moore Paint Company surely did. Plus, my house looked so darned pretty!

And there are other times that I can't seem to move myself out of that pain. I wallow in it like it's bathwater. I almost feel like I'm in a dreamlike state. I know I should be moving but I am at a standstill, blocked from taking any sort of action by a weight on my body and a fog in my mind. For that moment in time, I cannot remember feeling differently. I know that I have, but I just can't access the memory enough to feel comforted. I just sit in it.

And after I've managed to waste countless hours drowning in it and someone or something shakes me free, I then feel even worse because I've now got more and more things piled up on me. Will I ever learn? Oh, yes, maybe someday. What is it about pain that stifles us like that? I've explored this with clients and friends and I've found some answers. The comfort is that we all share some things in common with one another in this thing we call "life."

We all feel pain. We all get sidetracked. We all feel overwhelmed, misguided, frustrated, disillusioned, impatient, and like we just want to hit some magical button that makes all of that clamor in our heads cease. But, I've found through my work and my experience, that you "the only way out is through." You can't skip steps in that process any more than you can leave flour out of a cake. (And a note to all of the gluten-free, organic-only, farm-raised-products-only food experts: Yes, I suppose there's a way to make cake with no flour, but you get my point, right?)

~Hero~

When you think of a "hero," you most likely think of someone who has been dealt a raw deal yet stayed positive and thankful throughout the trials and tribulations they faced. That's my friend, Christine: A downright inspirational hero. After being diagnosed with stage 4 colon cancer, doctor after doctor concluded that she'd been delivered a death sentence.

As a beloved wife, daughter, and sister, and the mother of two school-aged daughters, she decided from jump that giving up was not an option. So, she searched for a doctor who would tell her something the others didn't: that she had a chance to beat it if she didn't give up. So that's exactly what she did. She never gave up. When her body was throwing in the towel, literally shutting down from organ to organ, she kept pushing forward. She returned for debilitating surgery after debilitating surgery, continuing to believe that her miracle was right around the corner. She spent countless days and nights in the hospital, or barely conscious at home. It was heartbreaking.

The absolutely beautiful thing was that every single time I visited with her, she had a sunny smile on her face and was always at the ready with a question about how I was doing. Like that mattered? Me? She was the one that needed to be given the attention. But she wanted to hear about my life so that she could take her mind off of her own troubles. She was sincerely grateful for the distraction that visitors offered. She refused to wallow in self-pity. And, boy, we would have understood completely if she had. She was overtaken by every possible challenge. All the cards kept getting stacked against her.

There were times that I saw her that the coloring in her face showed a person who was at death's door. I literally cried when I left her, thinking that it might have been the last time I'd see her. But Christine wasn't done with her life. And she was bound and determined to show her daughters that you fight when you face adversity, and that for every breath you are given, that you are deeply thankful for the gift of it. She struggled with anger sometimes. Wouldn't you? Her anger didn't turn into resentment and poison her. Instead it propelled her forward and reminded her *why* she was mad: Because she loved her life and wanted more time and more health. So when she had even a smidge of it, she grabbed it, celebrated it, and envisioned more.

And how has this turned out? Back in 2013, she was invited to take part in a study that was all about her recovery. She was seen as a cancer rock star, really. The doctors attributed the "miracle" (and it is that) she experienced in pushing a stage 4 diagnosis into remission in two years to her inspirational attitude and appreciation for every extra day she was given. She focused on the light that she could bring into the world and the not darkness that enveloped her. She directed all of her attention toward what was right in her world and the precious gifts of her family, friends, and just a simply sunny day.

Tragically, the cancer returned with a vengeance and quickly took her life. After the news, without hesitation, she continued to be positive, loving, giving, and a graceful example of the light we all wish to see in the world. She focused her attention and energy on the path, not the destination. We could learn a lot from her and happily skip the diagnosis. Simply put, a light shone into the darkness is comparatively that much brighter. Even, and especially, in the face of pain and uncertainty, bring hope and a smile and you and the world will be better for it.

~*Reaching Across Enemy Lines*~

What would happen if you shifted your thinking and started being appreciative of others, including those same individuals who make your life difficult? There is the age-old adage: "Keep your friends close, keep your enemies closer." Instead of just vilifying your "enemies," take some time to get to know something about them.

I challenge you to look for the good in and the things you have in common with those people who challenge you. Adopt an attitude of gratitude for their place in your world, even with the most difficult people. They are there to challenge you and make you grow, so seek that learning opportunity. When you recognize and validate them, even some small morsel of them, you are more open to see their struggle and be able to identify their unmet needs. See if you can figure out what their unmet needs are and do one little thing toward meeting them. Try it.

~*Thanking Your Enemies*~

First, I want you to reach across enemy lines and be sympathetic to people who are being pains in the rear to you and now I want you to *thank* your enemies? No, I haven't been smoking from the peace pipe. Well…no, seriously. I haven't! I swear! Okay, then you might be thinking, "is this woman out of her mind?" If I am, well, it's not for this reason. As a matter of fact, incorporating this (thanking my enemies) into my daily routine has been a saving grace in my life and helped me to hold onto sanity far longer than some predicted I could. I promise you that this is a vital lesson. It's tough, but core.

And you don't have to be a saint or pray on a mountain top surrounded by ancient music and religious role models to do this. It just requires an open mind and a willingness to try something new. When you do this (thank your enemies) on a consistent basis, you will reap countless benefits. Your sanity and happiness being the first two benefits. And, the world will move differently and for the better. Ready?

Let's stop for a minute and think about hate. Really think about it. I'm suggesting to downright *dwell* on it. Hate requires an excessive amount of energy. They say it takes many more muscles to frown than to smile; it takes exponentially more energy to hate than to love. You were made to love. To come from love. And, depending on your spiritual leanings, you will return to love. When you love it creates more feelings of love. The same holds true for hate. The more you hate, the more you hate. And, often, the more you are hated. Now, please don't misunderstand me: Love and hate are not opposite emotions. The opposite of <u>both</u> love and hate is indifference. Pure apathy. The lack of caring. Hate requires that we care. We often become preoccupied and downright obsessed with the object of our hatred.

Now, imagine reclaiming that energy and focus for something positive? Can I share a secret? You can. Right now. *Right now*.

Are you questioning how I've become an expert on this topic? That's a fair challenge, especially as you decide whether or not you should jump off this cliff and follow my advice. So, I'll tell you how.

Aside from studying people and relationships almost single-mindedly all of my life, I have been the hater and the hate-ee. I grew up with insecurity and rage (and some paranoia thrown in for extra fun) all around me. And I married into it. There was always someone to hate, a person to blame for some horrid transgression. Intolerance and passing judgment became my hallmarks just to fit in. It was toxic and I literally felt my spirit slowly dying under the weight of it.

Hate is heavy. And it doesn't let you go easily. It wants you to stay and create more of it. Feed it. When I left, it followed me. Only now I was the hate-ee. The hated one. And I still am. I am resigned to the fact that I will always be. Which is painful yet freeing at some level. I know that I cannot change it so I can release the pain of being on the receiving end of it. I know that it's not about *me*, but it is a reflection of the hater's pain and struggle. And I choose not to return it with more of the same. Those who hate and are mean are filled with it themselves. They are not clean and happy. They are filled with the emotional equivalent of toxic waste. Yuck.

Its remnants are disturbing. Just as you can feel the warmth of love in a room, you are frozen out by hatred. It touches everyone in its path. It is incredibly destructive. Hatred invites anxiety, fear, distrust, and sadness. It is exhausting and it slowly wrecks the house it lives in: The hater destroys him/herself from the inside out, slowly but surely.

So what does all of this have to do with validation? This section is called, "thanking your enemies," and to thank someone, you first must feel gratitude…and understanding and compassion. You appreciate something about them or something they've done. You recognize how they have helped you. You acknowledge that their behavior or mere presence benefits you. You validate their place in your life and the path they've walked. That's pretty easy to do when someone bakes you a cake or mows your lawn. It's a smidge harder when they do you harm. When they are literally wishing you dead. Trust me when I tell you that I know how that feels. And I believe that if I could find my way to appreciation, you can, too.

How do you get started? At the risk of sounding downright silly, come from a place of love when you thank your enemies. Maybe not the love you feel for them, but a loving place. Love, unlike hate, builds strength and energy. It brings peace of mind and happy. One of my favorite songs is "Good Morning" (by Chamillionaire) because one of the lines in the song is "I want to show all of my haters love." Haters, or those who wish you harm and failure, are neutralized by this approach because you remove the fight. There is nothing to argue about because you're taking away their power: You're refusing to engage in the hate war. You're checking out of the fight and deciding to act with compassion and concern. You can't have a tug-of-war if you're not holding the other end of the rope.

Did you ever stop to think about the extreme pain that a person is in who is actively hating others all the time? I know I feel the stress in my chest, my head, and the pit of my stomach. When I feel resentment and hatred for someone, I feel like I'm being set on fire from the inside out. Can you imagine feeling like that most minutes of most days? Ugh. That has got to be so painful. It's a private hell, really. And you know people who are living in it and you probably bump into them every day in the hallway.

When you attempt the mental and emotional gymnastics move of thanking a person like this, first think about how much pain they must be in. Focus on being compassionate for a person who is in that much soul-level pain. Come from that place in your message: Their actions are the result of their pain. And when they act terribly toward you, it's not a reflection of *you*, it's a direct reflection of *them*. Because you wouldn't behave that way, would you? Happy and confident people don't hurt other people intentionally, they build people up. So, build people up (even and especially those you've shared hate with), feeling compassion for those in too much pain to do so.

Did you ever try to be your best self when you're experiencing a migraine? People who are consumed with hatred have the equivalent of a full-body migraine every minute of every day. They certainly are accountable for the choice to hate, but breaking that viscous cycle is tough and their hatred typically blinds them to the opportunity to be any other way. "Forgive them, Father, for they know not what they do" (Luke 23:34) fits this perfectly. Hate blinds people. Forgive them for their actions that originate in this blindness.

Exercise: Thank An Enemy

Step 1: Be clear and honest about how *you* may be being hateful to the other person. Think about how you may be feeding into the war you're in and the hate that you may be feeling, too. Listen for how many times you've said to yourself, "but they deserved it!" Vow to end that behavior because you recognize how destructive it is. Let go of thinking that their hate and hateful actions toward you are about who **you** are. Instead, know that their behavior describes who **they** are. And you know this because your actions do not describe another person and who **they** are: They describe who **you** are.

Step 2: Like Batman and the Joker, think of who you would be and what would define you if they weren't in your life? Certainly think of the good stuff that makes you wish they would evaporate into thin air, but also think of how your life and sense of yourself might change if they did. As an example, being a hate-ee has tested my determination, my positivity, and my endurance. Without his (the hater's) presence, I wouldn't be able to define myself and my actions in opposition to his. In other words, he gives me the room to be a better person because I have to not collapse under the weight of his hate. And, his tests provide me with a view of how strong and resilient I am.

Step 3: Put your validation for the hater into words. Write things like, "Thank you for making me appreciate the loving people in my world. I am grateful for the tests you continue to give to me because they offer me the chance to prove my strength. Thank you for showing me in living color the kind of person I don't want to be, the opportunity to be resolute in staying positive and happy no matter what you do to hurt me." And keep going. Create your own personalized ones. And leave the sarcasm at the door. There are truly things to be grateful for when someone is a hater toward you. Let yourself feel the thanks. By honoring it, you honor yourself and you diminish their negative influence and power over your life. Do you really want them to have power over you? Does that feel good? Then complete this exercise and take back your power, peacefully.

If you want to live longer, healthier, happier, and more abundantly, let go of hate. Replace hate with validation. It may sound impossible, but it's not. It requires persistence and practice, but it comes with time. And every small effort toward that end builds your strength and resolve to keep going. As they teach in physics class, objects in motion tend to stay in motion, so get moving. There is no time like the present to hate less and be grateful more and that takes action on your part. To hold onto hate is to be in perpetual pain. Pain does have its upside, as long as you don't make it the center of your existence and you let it teach you how to be a better person.

As you learned in this book, if someone has unmet needs, they have a source of pain and discomfort and their actions can be traced back to efforts at feeding those needs. If that person was your friend, how would you help him/her? Once you figure out what those unmet needs are, you can use the insights and strategies you found in this book to guide them toward meeting them. And you can take your own action steps to do the same to help them. And you will help yourself in the process. It just doesn't get much better than that.

"Life is to be enjoyed, not endured" ~Gordon B. Hinckley

Validation

~End of Chapter Inventory~

"When you don't come from struggle,
gaining appreciation is a quality that is hard to come by."
~ Shania Twain

Summary: Feeling validated is central to our emotional and psychological well-being. And experiencing a consistent level of gratitude fosters positive attitudes and relationships.

Key Concepts:

- When you don't feel validated, you often act in destructive and needy ways.
- You can choose to be grateful, even for challenges.
- When you stop feeling guilty for being happy, the world gets better.

What are three takeaways you have from this chapter? What did you learn about yourself and/or others? What shifts in thinking did you experience as a result of reading this chapter?

Takeaway 1:

Takeaway 2:

Takeaway 3:

***Rate yourself on your confidence and competence practicing
the key concepts in this chapter:***

1: I'm so lousy I don't want to respond

2

3

4

5: I'm okay, but I have a lot to learn

6

7

8

9

10: I'm going to write my own book on this competency

***What are three things you commit to do (differently) as a
result of reading this chapter?*** Think of things that will improve
your life personally, spiritually, emotionally, and physically.

Commitment 1:

Commitment 2:

Commitment 3:

***What are three roadblocks/challenges to being where you
need to be?*** What are three things (relationships, habits, assumptions,

situations) that you need to adjust and/or remove in order to live happier?

Roadblock 1:

Roadblock 2:

Roadblock 3:

What are three strategies for addressing those roadblocks and challenges? What are three changes you could make that would reduce or remove the obstacles you have?

Strategy 1:

Strategy 2:

Strategy 3:

"Think of all the beauty still left around you
and be happy." ~ Anne Frank

PASSION & PURPOSE

"Twenty years from now you will be more disappointed by the things
that you didn't do than by the ones you did do.
So throw off the bowlines. Sail away from the safe harbor.
Catch the trade winds in your sails.
Explore. Dream. Discover." ~ H. Jackson Brown, Jr.

People, in general, have a lack of passion in their lives. Those who
have their fair share of passion are likely on the cover of a magazine or
on television or blazing trails in some other venue. That just leaves the
other 99.4% of us to stumble through each day, longing for something
that we can't even put a label on most of the time.

The object of that longing is passion and purpose: To feel an energy
for something. A reason for existing and plowing through the ups and
downs of daily life. To want something with vigor and the knowledge
that you were put on this earth to drive toward it. Knowing that you
have a reason for living and wanting to live that purpose out with
enthusiasm.

But too many of us are floundering, simply existing, with no "true
north" to guide us toward anything. We're "just not that into"
anything. It's just day-to-day drudgery that holds our attention. What
homework we have to work on, what time practice is tomorrow,

whether or not that cute guy/girl will pay any attention to us, what to wear to the party this weekend, and whether or not we've gotten all our chores done at home. The devil really is in the details, and we are breathing, eating, and sleeping with the devil.

Where is the fire in our bellies? Do you remember when you were a little kid and people asked you what you wanted to be when you grew up? Do you remember what you told them? Was it an exciting, high-profile, maybe even heroic career? Maybe you wanted to be a firefighter? Teacher? Doctor? Lawyer? Ballerina? I've met my share of kids who said, "Superman!" or "Wonder Woman!" I haven't met a person who remembers saying anything about a life spent "getting through each day."

No, that wasn't for you! You wanted fun, intrigue, excitement, reward, happiness, and two more elements that you probably couldn't name way back then: purpose and passion. You wanted to exist for a reason. You wanted to bring value to the world. You wanted to entertain or help others through doing what you do best, by sharing your passion for something. To you, possibilities were endless and happiness is something you got if you wanted it and put your heart into it. The world was your oyster.

It still is. The world is literally at your feet each and every day. No, it doesn't matter what grade you got on your last chemistry exam. Or if you just got dumped by a friend or love interest. Or if you have no clue as to what you want to be when you grow up. There are endless choices open to you, even if you can't see them clearly now. If you'd asked me when I was 14 if I'd be a leadership coach and motivational speaker and educator I'd have laughed, clueless as to what that even *meant*. It's okay not to know, just please do me a favor: Don't shut off chances to follow paths that excite you.

So many adults I meet have lost their way to finding and living that passion. And these adults may likely include your parents, teachers, and other pivotal adults in your life. Were we so naïve or have we lost something along the way? My money is on option number two. We forgot how to hold onto our passion. We lost our belief that we are all equipped for joy and celebration. We ignored our vision for a life of freedom and opportunity and replaced it with commitments and obligations that tethered us to an existence, not a life. So how can you prevent this from happening to you?

~What Do You Want?~

An existence? Is that all that you want? Is that truly what you want to have for as long as you're still here on this planet? Tomorrow is promised to no one. When I went through my own near-death experience, I assessed my life. Being forced to acknowledge my own mortality up-close and personal was jarring, but it gave me a sense of how far off the mark my life was. I was compromising my own essence for the <u>appearance</u> of happiness and fulfillment. I was neither happy nor fulfilled. I'd sold out.

Once I realized that my time on Earth was truly limited (and maybe even severely limited), I woke up and I took inventory. I made changes and shifted my thinking. I began a better relationship with myself and the ones I loved. I figured out what I could do for a living that was a life and not a chore. I set my sights on doing more things that would put more of me and my essence into the world, for its benefit. And you can do these things, too.

What's that saying? "Today is the first day of the rest of your life." It surely is. So what are you going to do with today? How are you going to light that fire in your belly to move you forward? How are you going to motivate yourself to find your purpose and your passion? Will you take on that challenge? No one can live it for you except you. Not your parents. Not anyone but *you*.

Are you going to let the barriers you perceive stop you from living the life you've imagined? You can blame your parents or your circumstances all day long but they won't be living your life: *You will*. Live the darn thing already, would you?! Need help? Then ask for it. Be in the driver's seat of your own life…no one else can do it for you!

~Passion and Purpose~

"We're not broken, just bent, and we can learn to love again." ~ Pink

Passion requires having a purpose; loving something and wanting to see it succeed, expand, and take up more space in the world. Your purpose could be highly interpersonal and focused on relationships, (like teaching or being a parent) or more focused on results (like inventing things or writing). When you have a purpose, you plug into the energy that is available in the Universe, just like an electrical current. You are literally conducting energy. People who hear you share your purpose say things like, "you just lit up" or "you're on fire."

Some of us are actually attentive enough to literally feel your energy and we are energized. We want to carry that energy into the world and do something with it. Imagine a world with more passionate people and the multiplier effect produced, sending currents of inspiration, initiative, and connection everywhere. What the world truly needs is more passionate people. So how do you grab ahold of your passion? It's easy: Start with your purpose.

~*Figuring Out Your Purpose*~

"Your purpose in life is to find your purpose
and give your whole heart and soul to it."
~ Gautama Buddha

Before you can get passionate about much of anything you need to get clarity on your purpose. Why you were put here and what you can to do put more of "you" into the world? As I was writing this book, a client passed along a quote that he heard that went something like this, "Hell is getting to Heaven and being shown who you could have been if only you'd better used the gifts you were given." This was a "WOW" moment for me.

Pause on this message for a minute because it's a critical message. I mean it, a whole minute. Go back and read the quote again then close your eyes, take some deep breaths, and don't start reading again until you've let that one sink in. Need another minute? Take it. Using the gifts you were given is the cornerstone of our lives here. And you won't get much mileage out of this book if you don't own this concept. Please know that it'll present some struggles. It'll shake you up a bit, for certain, but once you get it, you will be transformed. Growth involves discomfort, but it is worth it. Adolescence is so much about finding out *who you are* and *what you want to do* with your life. Use this time to take the reigns and look into yourself and appreciate the gifts you have. The things that make you uniquely you. It doesn't mean you have to be "the best" at anything. They are simply things that you find joy and satisfaction in doing.

Do you know what your gifts are? Do you have any idea what you're supposed to be doing here except breathing in and out air and taking up space on this crowded planet of ours? Maybe you stumbled into a moment when you knew with clarity what you were put here to do and to be? For those of you who have, congratulations! That is rare and special. For those of you who haven't, get ready. You're about to discover it. If you already know, well, please bear with me because I might challenge your assumptions...so follow me.

> The real issue in life is not how many blessings we have,
> but what we do with our blessings.
> Some people have many blessings and hoard them.
> Some have few and give everything away." ~ Mister Rogers

Now it's time to write down some things about you that you are good at, enjoy doing, are sought out for by friends and family members as skills and talents, etc. These can be tangible things (e.g., "fixing things" and "organizing projects") or intangible things (e.g., "understanding people" and "inspiring others"). Don't judge them. Just let the thoughts flow.

My Gifts Are:

1.

2.

3.

4.

5.

"Pleasure in the job puts perfection in the work."
~ Aristotle

I was sitting in the local coffee and lunch hot spot in my town, waiting to meet up with someone to see if our businesses could work well together. An older guy was walking past me and as he saw me sitting alone and fiercely taking notes, he stopped and said, "Work, work, work." And his tone wasn't like the seven dwarfs with a spring in his step and a whistle on his lips. No, this was the mantra of a man who saw work as burden and distraction from "real" life. I looked at him, and in my incurably optimistic tone, said, "YES! I'm so blessed to be able to work, and to love what I do!"

He stopped short, intrigued, I'm sure, since most people would have nodded at him and grumbled, "Yeah" and gone right back to the pain of their project. My response surprised him. To satisfy his curiosity, he asked me what I did for a living. I said, "I help people find their passion and purpose so that they can live more authentically, communicate more openly, and resolve their conflict more healthfully."

It seems this sounded pretty cool to him because his face lit up like the Fourth of July and he immediately shared a story about his wife and how miserable she was in her job and how she could really use some help. We spoke for another minute or two and I shared some advice and tidbits (and my business card) for his wife's benefit until the person I was scheduled to meet with arrived.

Do you want a job that you could speak about like that? Have you ever found yourself excited about a project or experience like that? What made it different from the others? What was the mission of it? Was it consistent with what you wanted to put into the world? Did you understand your mission and like it? Was it easy to get up in the morning to do the work required?

The reason I was able to knock this guy's mental socks off with my enthusiasm was because I am thoroughly committed to the mission of my work and I am sincerely passionate about what I do. In order to have passion flowing through you and energizing your spirit, you need to live and work with a purpose. I can't tell you how many people I run into that do not have a firm grasp of the mission for which they are investing 40, 50, 60, 70 or more hours a week of their lives.

Once you figure out what makes you passionate, do whatever it takes to hold onto that passion. Don't compromise what you want to do in this world for what you're "expected" to do or you'll waste part of your life chasing a dream that isn't yours. This is *your* life. *Your* story. Tell it.

~My Story~

For me, I figured out why I exist when I faced not existing at all. I was 32 and had held some jobs to that point that did invigorate me, but my life overall was just holding up the status quo and keeping up appearances. I wasn't really living with joy and from a position of abundance. And then everything changed for me. I was faced head-on with my own mortality and life all of a sudden came into sharp focus. I couldn't ignore my soul's unrest anymore.

Like with most journeys, I believe that I was on the path before I recognized the stones that lay before and behind me. For the past ten years, I have made my living as a life and executive coach and leadership trainer so I have recounted the story of the discovery and pursuit of my life purpose countless times. And all of those times have been with pleasure and peace, knowing that in sharing my story, I am helping my clients to find their own place in this world.

In 2003, I got pregnant with my second child. I was working from home raising my first born, a little girl, and finding it challenging to balance earning an income and making a life as a wife and mother. I had a lot of stress in my life, and I was very sick for the first five months of the pregnancy. When I was six and a half months pregnant (four days before the anniversary of my father's death), I had a stroke. The neurologist tested me for a brain tumor, multiple sclerosis, and lupus. She thought it was a stroke but she had to eliminate the other disorders before she could be sure. In my precocious and somewhat controlling fashion, I made it clear to the doctors that I was voting for "stroke." When friends called me in the hospital after the medical verdict was in, I happily announced that I had a stroke. Because I knew that it was a medical blessing of sorts. I didn't see at the time that the stroke would end up changing my whole life.

The doctors watched me, and my unborn child, very closely for the remainder of my pregnancy, knowing that my life or my pregnancy could end at any moment. We made it through the pregnancy, but then the delivery day arrived. It was a fast birth, and my body was not equipped to handle it. I hemorrhaged and was not staying conscious very long, even with medical intervention. Because of the stroke during my pregnancy, the doctors did not want to give me a clotting agent, but they were running out of options.

Luckily, my body and the medicine and treatments worked together and I came out of the woods and was finally able to hold my baby daughter. In that moment, I knew that something in my life was going to change, something profound and long-lasting. It was going to be a fork in the road, full of new beginnings and endings.

Over the next few months, I left myself open to discovering what job could allow me to continue to work from home and have infrequent separations from my children. After watching an organizing show, I was inspired to investigate that career. I spoke with professional organizers in my market and decided that this would be my best option given how much money I could make in just a few hours a week.

It became clear that I was doing so much more than organizing in my work with my clients: I was helping people to realign their relationship to "things" so that they could more fully embrace their relationship to themselves and to other people.

I discovered that I was a "relationship coach" and clients started referring friends and relatives to me to coach them in all aspects of their lives. I found that the common element to my work with each client was bringing them to recognize and attend to their "essence," the characteristics that made them who they were. In that process, they could then discover what activities and experiences made them passionate about life and that translated into their purpose in life. I began teaching "strategic life planning" to audiences big and small, with the intention of getting the message of discovering one's *life purpose* as an essential element to living any kind of life on this planet.

This was a new beginning for me: A time when I was becoming who I was meant to be and able to offer my true essence to my clients. As with any beginning, it marked the end of something as well. It led to the end of my marriage. My medical scare during my second pregnancy brought me to value my life in a way I never had before. And my new career was allowing me to appreciate myself in a new way, as well. This combination of "happy" provided a sharp contrast to the suffocating and abusive marriage I had committed my life to, knowingly from the beginning.

But, I had made a decision to live the life I was meant to live and to honor God by loving myself and others as He loved me. This forced a choice: To leave and take all the risks that a divorce presents, or stay and slowly let my spirit continue to die. It took me years to come to terms with this, but I did, and I left, and I stayed gone. Every time I feared that I had made the wrong decision, I reminded myself that I could not remain in a marriage that would suffocate the life I was meant to live. And, I gave my kids a mom they would never have had if I'd stayed. I'm the true "me" now and I truly believe that they need *me*. This gave me peace, as did my clients who wrestled with change decisions of their own and then used our work together to transform their own lives into intentional, passionate, and purposeful ones.

For the past number of years, even amidst a very protracted and conflicted divorce, I am clear every moment of every day that I am doing exactly what I was put on this Earth to do: to guide, to inspire, and to connect. In my former jobs and in my marriage I could not do any of those, or to such a minimal level that they weren't worth doing at all. With this clarity, I can make purposeful decisions and take passionate actions to follow my path wherever it may lead me. All the while, I know that the beauty of this is that the journey *is* the destination.

So what did I learn from all of this? It's simple: I learned the transformational power of passion. If you don't got it, you gotta go and get it.

~Whatever You Do, Do It With Passion.~

A client of mine is a runner. You know the type. He gets up at o'dark thirty to run some ridiculous distance in rain, sleet, snow, or wind to stay in tip-top athlete shape. A runner. Not like me who "ran" one summer in order to drop a few pounds. Aside from weight loss, the only reason I could come up with to run was if I was being chased. And even then I'd just hope fate intervened and I could grab a ride somehow. He's not a "runner" like me. He's a real runner. He actually looked forward to catching a run. I don't know if it was the endorphins or being in good shape or what, but he loved running and didn't see it as torment (that would be me).

Now, back to my running client. On our coaching call one day, we were talking about the last time that he felt an overwhelming sense of happy and oneness with the world. In response, he shared with me some details about his morning run. He was running and he made a conscious effort to smile as he ran. Not a small grin, but a big toothy smile.

If you've ever noticed, runners don't tend to smile. They wince. They grit their teeth. They're on a mission: to survive the run. Aside from having painful dental work done, they look like they couldn't be suffering much more. Now, I don't know about you, but this is not a good recruitment tactic to get other people to tie their laces and hit the streets.

My client is of a different breed altogether. He's not a conformist. He's not run of the mill. He's daring, unique, and, *passionate*. He also observed that runners look miserable and decided that he was not going to be *that* kind of runner. He was going to be *his* breed of runner: He was going to enjoy himself and make sure that the world knew it. So he smiled, widely. And this little social experiment of his was met with some strange looks; of bewilderment, of curiosity, and sometimes of amusement. He even got a few return smiles. The first morning of his experiment he ran further and stronger than usual, and he returned invigorated instead of exhausted. So he kept it up. He's still running regularly, and he's still smiling throughout.

Is that how you run? Is that how you do anything? Have you ever tried dancing and singing your way through your daily chores? No, I'm not kidding. Imagine waking up on a Saturday morning with a long series of things on your "chores" list, and instead of groaning and wanting to crawl under a rock rather than face the list, you jump out of bed with a smile on your face. You turn on your favorite music playlist, crank up the volume, and start at it. You see if you can get a chore done before the end of a song. You be-bop around the house, vacuuming to the beat of the music. You dance while you scrub. Mopping to music is an experience, trust me. Got the visual yet?

You're having so much fun that your family members may offer help to you. You've turned obligations into an opportunity for fun.

You've become a poster child for not letting life drag you down, but instead lift you up. Think you'll get everything done quicker? You bet you will. And you'll have energy in reserves to do other things. You'll plow through that list of "must dos" and move right onto the "want tos." And you won't feel stressed and burdened. Is there a downside? Not one that comes even close to the upside. Counting the days until Saturday, aren't you?

If you can do your household chores with passion and enthusiasm, what about the rest of your life? Where else could you stand to infuse some of that energy? In your schoolwork? In your extracurriculars? In your relationships? Where should you start? I'm a big proponent of starting small and building things up. If you jump in and try to do everything differently, you might not recognize yourself and that cosmic shift might be enough to throw you back to the starting line. Everything all at once can be shocking to you and to everyone around you.

And other people's responses will surely affect you. You might surprise people and they may have been comfortable with you just the way you were. So they might work against you, in subtle ways or in overt ones. Maybe they'll tease you, telling you to "tone it down." Or maybe they'll add more to your plate so it'll be harder for you to be light and cheerful. If you start small and add in some passion to one activity at a time, you'll find less resistance. We don't tend to notice subtle shifts and are slow to react to them. It's like boiling a frog. Drop him in boiling water and he'll jump. Place him in a pot of cool water and slowly boil it and he'll stay put. We react to sudden change, too. If you want lasting change, introduce it slowly and keep at it. You can do this. So do it.

~Relationships & Passion: For Dating Teens~

There are literally thousands of human emotions that we have words for, but of the ones we experience on a routine basis, we can count that number on our fingers. Of those, about half (at best) are negative emotions. What's your North Star (the place you tend to aim for)? Happy? Angry? Sad? Cheerful? Do you know people whose excitement is contagious? When they speak about something that is important to them you want to learn more, experience more? People hear them and stop what they are doing to pay attention because the energy is magnetic. That's passion. It's love, but love with energy and enthusiasm.

We love lots of things and people in our lives if we're lucky. But love can be static. Unfortunately, so many of our "loving" relationships lack the energy behind the feeling of love. We say we "love" them but it doesn't move or change or inspire us to be any certain way. It just exists. It just *is*. It's like a warm blanket: Comforting, but once you're warm, it's just there. Passion can't just exist. Passion moves and changes and transforms the things that it touches. It brings in light and energy and inspiration. It's not a blanket. It's fire. It burns in you, propelling you toward that which you may not even be able to see. It can, and should, be life changing. Why might this sound foreign to you?

Because, sadly, it's not so common in our world. Unless it's about a sports team or political figure, over time we've gotten passion kicked out of us. We've been trained not to get our hopes up. Not to be too intense or we might upset someone. Not to rejoice too much or we might get embarrassed or make someone else feel left out. We might risk not being "cool." If we're passionate about something, often it's in the shadows, in the corners of our lives. We've watched our parents and many of them are like zombies (on a good day). That'll suck the life right out of you, won't it?

In our relationships, a lack of passion is a killer. Many relationships end because we hop to another one looking for more excitement, sometimes cheating before we go. Why are people cheating or trading in relationships like they mean nothing? The list of reasons varies, but from what I've found, and experienced, it comes from a need for passion, a demand for that energy and connection. Passion is life giving. Passion makes you feel like you're ready to take on the world. For those of you who have cheated or jumped ship, does this sound familiar? Did you stray because you needed to feel more alive? Were you nearly dead and needed life support, or were you energized and wanted to move on because your relationship was "dead?" Were you just plain bored?

Plugging into the energy and clarity that passion provides, we can finally recognize our own power and potential. Considering your core relationships, try answering the following questions: Why are you there, in that relationship? What does it bring to you and what do you bring to it? Without purpose there can be no passion. If you're in a serious relationship, what's your purpose in being in your relationship? The teen years are the proving ground for your adult relationships, so take advantage of these experiences to learn more about yourself, your boyfriend/girlfriend, and what you want out of a relationship. Some of our teen relationships last well into adulthood, so pouring the right foundation is critical.

"Love, it will not betray you, dismay or enslave you.
It will set you free." ~ Mumford & Sons

~My "First Love" Story~

I got engaged for the first time (don't ask how many times, lol) when I was 17. I was a freshman in college and I was madly in love. I'd had a lot of turmoil growing up and finding "home" with a boyfriend was almost too good to be true. When he asked me to marry him I was so freaking happy I thought I was going to explode! Someone wanted to marry me? Someone I loved? Holy crap! I said, "yes" and we planned a beautiful wedding for the following summer, right after I turned 18.

As we were ordering the wedding invitations, I freaked out. Getting married went from being a romantic thought to a reality and I panicked. I broke off the engagement and we broke up. It was a really sad time in my life and I felt terribly for years about hurting him. Decades later we bumped into each other on Facebook and had a conversation about his side of the story which was eye-opening. He knew we were too young to get married but he fell so deeply in love with me that he was afraid if he didn't propose that he might lose me. He thought that getting married was the best way to hold onto me. Pretty crazy, right? At the time, it seemed perfectly reasonable to get married. It was the way to keep that passion! I'm pretty sure it was also the way to ensure that we got divorced if we'd gone through with it. If you're racing toward that level of seriousness in your relationships, let your foot off the gas for a second. Just pause. If it's meant to be, it can take a pause. When you're racing (desperately) toward something you miss a lot of signs along the way.

Wouldn't it be good to know how your definition of "happy" fits with your boyfriend/girlfriend's? To feed the needs that both of you have for passion and connection, without rushing to get married to feel safe like I almost did. How can you do that?

- The first step is *Discovery*, or finding out what makes you and your boyfriend/girlfriend happy and what feeds each of your needs.
- The second step is *Negotiation*, or coming to some agreement with your boyfriend/girlfriend as to what you can each do to feed one another's needs.
- The third step is *Implementation*, or feeding those needs with intentional, authentic, and caring action.
- The fourth and final step is *Evaluation*, or coming to terms with what's working and what's not.

Both people must be honest with themselves and one another as to what they need and what they are willing to offer. You can't smile and shine the other person on, pretending it's all better or that you don't mind stretching yourself to feed their needs. That won't last long and resentment is sure to sink into your relationship, destroying it from the inside out. Be courageous and be honest with yourself and your boyfriend/girlfriend or you'll be trapped behind a mask and won't feel the joy of a deep connection.

Which brings me right to the "bad" news. Sometimes in the evaluation step, even if all of the other steps were done with caring and willingness, you may find that there is a lack of fit between what one of you needs and what the other is capable of giving. You want one depth of connection and the other person is satisfied with a casual relationship. And you <u>cannot</u> change the other person. Do I need to repeat myself? You cannot change them. Regardless of how charming, insightful, inspiring, and powerful you may be, you cannot change another person. You cannot make them feel what you feel. You cannot make them want what you want. You can invite them to, but you cannot make it so. That old adage, "you can lead a horse to water but you can't make him drink" holds true for us two-legged creatures, too.

Feel free to show them what you want, to share your vision of happiness, but don't think for a second that you can make them submit to your will. Oh, they may stay in that space for some time if you insist on trying to control them. For the good of security, fitting in, and the status quo, you might not lose them on the surface. But sure as the sun will rise in the morning, you will lose them underneath, on the levels that should matter in a relationship. Like a dog tied up outside, he will find a way to chew through his leash and break free. So, focus on you, on what you can change, on what you can give to the relationship.

Communicate with love. Come from love, not judgment and hostility, in all that you say. Model the way. Resist the urge to do the work for him/her. Let go of the fantasy that you can make it different all by yourself. You cannot. There are two people in a relationship, not one. If you're going to try to do the work for you and them, you might as well be alone. It's less frustrating that way, trust me.

Bottom line: If you want passion, be passionate. If you want more love, be more loving. If you want to be more inspired, act more inspiring. If you want to be understood, inquire and listen more. If you want to have your needs fed, feed more needs. Offer what you seek. Give what you most want. You may not always get what you give, but you will get so much more of what you give if you give more. It is that simple and that hard.

~Claiming Your Own Stoke~

What do you want to be when you grow up? How can you be passionate about it? How can you live the life you were meant to live? How can you create the career that will allow you to express who you are and to give the most of yourself? Try this next exercise and you'll be on your way.

Exercise

Think back to a time you felt truly energetic about something. Maybe it was a special project at school. Perhaps it was a volunteer assignment. Or it might have been a relationship. The hallmark of it is that it filled you with energy, with drive, with enthusiasm. You couldn't wait to get to it, to make progress with it, to bring it to the next level, and to watch it grow.

Now write it down. Describe it and how it made you feel. What were some of its key characteristics? How did it bring out the best in you? Try to limit it to 3-5 words. Say those words over and over again to see how you feel when you hear yourself claim them. Share them with others. See how they fit. This is a big deal so treat it as such. If you want fire in your belly, you need passion in your soul. This is the first big step to find it.

This exercise will lead you to discovering your purpose, your "why." And I can't say enough how critical that is to finding satisfaction and joy in your life. So get to it!

"Finding the right work is like discovering your own soul in the world." ~Thomas Moore

161

~*Warning!*~

You might be thinking that when you identify your core purpose you're going to have to make over your whole life: Quit school, move out, change your name, and maybe go live in a tree. While you might feel compelled to make one or more of these choices, none of them are necessary. The way you live a life of passion is to have a purpose in what you do. To know, to claim, and to live out your WHY.

You could be a tax accountant or a movie star and have the very same purpose; you'll simply express your "why" differently through your "how." My life's purpose is to guide, to inspire, and to connect. Each and every element of this purpose is easily manifested in my work as a leadership consultant, coach, speaker, trainer, and author. And most of all: A mom.

But, let's say that I spent a huge chunk of my life (and invested a heap of money getting educated) as a rocket scientist at NASA. Now that I've read this passage on purpose I start to panic. What does guiding, inspiring, and connecting have to do with rocket science? Rocket science is the "what" that I do. The "why" I do it needs to be my purpose (guide, inspire, and connect). The "how" requires creativity.

Maybe I expand my job to include training new employees or offering talks to tourists or aspiring engineers? That might take care of all three elements of my purpose. Or maybe I work hard to lead my team and channel my purpose that way. In making changes to live the life you were meant to live, a total overhaul isn't required. It might be, but chances are that you can, at least for the time being, stay right where you are. You're just going to adjust your focus. Modify your perspective on the "why." Adapt your interpretations (thoughts) and approaches (actions). You got this.

"The only thing standing between you and your goal is the bullshit story you keep telling yourself as to why you can't achieve it."
~ Jordan Belfort

~Passion & Teen Leaders~

"Don't you think it's better to be extremely happy for a short while,
even if you lose it, than to be just okay for your whole life?"
~ Audrey Niffenegger, *The Time Traveler's Wife*

In this chapter, you read about how to find your passion and purpose and what it has to do with your overall identity. This next segment will address what you, as a leader, have influence over in terms of building passion for your organization's benefit. Do you have a club you're a leader for? Or have you thought about running for an office in a club you're in? Feeding the need for passion in an organization is like holding the Holy Grail in your grasp. It marks the difference between an average group and an epic organization. Which one would you like to be in?

What can you do, as a leader, to give your members a jump start to live with passion and purpose and to attract the very best people and resources to it? First and foremost, you need to make sure that the organization has an established mission ("why" it exists) that is communicated to everyone connected to it in any way. Every member must be able to tell others why the organization exists. And further, they should be able to communicate what their role is in accomplishing that mission. Do they know what that role is? Do they have any clue as to how their work contributes to the mission, to the purpose of the organization? Why does it takes up space on the planet?

Disney might have a goal to bring 2,400,000 people through their parks next year or to create shareholder wealth, but neither of those are their mission. Their core mission is to create happiness. If you ask any of their employees ("cast members") you'll hear that same message over and over again. You might hear them add words like "magical" and "memorable," but they all know what they are there for: To create happiness.

Why does this make a difference? If everyone at Disney knows that their central responsibility is to create happiness, you could assume that they are rewarded for doing so. You could also guess that they are given the tools to accomplish that mission. And, that they feel a passion for succeeding, whether for intrinsic or extrinsic reasons. If a Disney employee had a decision to make on the job, the employee would know right up front that the value of creating happiness was above all others (unless it was safety, since you can't be too happy if you're hospitalized). Decision making is made so much easier. Communication is simpler since everyone is coming from the same organizing principle: To do whatever is necessary and seek out whatever possible resources and experiences to create happiness. There are fewer disagreements and more rallying around their common agenda.

This is why so many organizations around the world try to emulate Disney. Disney seems to have a secret that no one else has been able to crack the code on. Yet, it seems pretty simple: Have a purpose that your members can feel good about, talk about, and embody in their daily responsibilities. When people know their purpose and it's consistent with their core values, it ignites passion. It creates a situation where they want to invest their time, energy, and resources into helping the organization reach their core purpose: To live their mission through their work.

What if your members are bored being part of your organization? What if they don't have any passion for it and they don't even know what the group mission is? How likely are they to promote the joining it to their friends? Not likely. Who wants to bring their friends into a lame group and then get grief for it?

On the other hand, what if your members know and love the mission? In that case, you've got yourself some unpaid spokespeople who are naturally talking up your organization because they love being there. When you're passionate about something, you tend to not want to shut up about it. Which, in this particular case, benefits the group because it attracts people who are excited about becoming a part of it. They are invested in it because they have witnessed how much their friend has gained from being a part of it: Energy versus exhaustion, excitement versus stress, and passion over boredom.

So how can you tap into your natural passion so that you will be motivated to go out and set the world on fire? What will ignite your passion? Remember: It's not the "what," it's the "why." Why you do what you do is what gets you up in the morning and keeps you up late at night. The "what" is just the details of the thing you're doing which could change week to week or year to year. If you decide to be a nurse (your "what") someday because you want to help to heal people (your "why"), you could be a therapist (your "what") without changing your why. Get it? Don't go crazy trying to figure out the "how." With a legitimate and inspiring "why," you'll figure out the how.

And that's the solid gold nugget that I hope you gathered, if nothing else in this whole chapter: When you have a why, you figure out the how. If your passion for a purpose is strong, you have the ability to move mountains to live that purpose. With passion and purpose you will be a living example of the infamous words of Christopher Robin:

"You are braver than you believe,
stronger than you seem, and
smarter than you think."

Passion

~End of Chapter Inventory~

"He who has a why to live can bear almost any how."
~ Friedrich Nietzsche

Summary: To share how passion affects our relationships and our results and how we can influence its presence in our lives.

Key Concepts:

- Figuring out your core purpose is a simple process.
- When we know what our purpose is, we can build a passionate connection to it.
- When passion is missing, we suffer and we have more stress, anxiety, and unhappiness.
- Our connections are superficial, unfulfilling, and open to threat if they are missing some level of passion.

What are three takeaways you have from this chapter? What did you learn about yourself and/or others? What shifts in thinking did you experience as a result of reading this chapter?

Takeaway 1:

Takeaway 2:

Takeaway 3:

Rate yourself on your confidence and competence practicing the key concepts in this chapter:

1: I'm so lousy I don't want to respond

2

3

4

5: I'm okay, but I have a lot to learn

6

7

8

9

10: I'm going to write my own book on this competency

What are three things you commit to do (differently) as a result of reading this chapter? Think of things that will improve your life personally, spiritually, emotionally, and physically.

Commitment 1:

Commitment 2:

Commitment 3:

What are three roadblocks/challenges to being where you need to be? What are three things (relationships, habits, assumptions, situations) that you need to adjust and/or remove in order to live happier?

Roadblock 1:

Roadblock 2:

Roadblock 3:

What are three strategies for addressing those roadblocks and challenges? What are three changes you could make that would reduce or remove the obstacles you have?

Strategy 1:

Strategy 2:

Strategy 3:

"Give a man a fire and he's warm for a day,
but set fire to him and he's warm
for the rest of his life." ~ Terry Pratchett

CONCLUDING THOUGHTS

"In three words I can sum up everything I've learned about life:
It goes on." ~ Robert Frost

Now what? You've spent some time reading this book and thinking about how it applies to you and those in your world. If you're the compliant and/or motivated type you've already completed the activities in and assessments at the end of each chapter. You may have shared some of your reflections, observations, thoughts, and feelings with some of your friends. You may have used some of the stories and examples with them to help them along their way. Did you try thinking about something differently than you did before you picked up the book? Did you do something in a different way than before? C'mon, admit it! You've been practicing staying in your "bubble" to stay out of crazy town, haven't you?

So, what do you do next?

More of the same. Just keep thinking and doing things differently and very soon you will have significantly changed your world. It's the butterfly effect: The flap of a butterfly's wings can create a wind event halfway around the world. Baby steps move you forward. If you're one who leaps, go for it. If not, do a little at a time. Just keep doing it. Don't stop. They say it takes six weeks to develop a new habit. Give the lessons and awakenings in this book six weeks to take hold and you'll find yourself with habits that will change your life for the better.

When your life gets better, life gets better for those around you, if they are willing to accept responsibility for their reaction and response to your changes. If they are inclined to blame and control, you may have some unhappy campers around you for some time. Whatever you do, don't let that be the reason you slide back into old, unhealthy habits. It might be hard, but you can hold the change in the face of challenge. The whole point of this book is to teach you how to have healthier and happier relationships, no matter what other people do.

What are you waiting for? Go grab the life you were intended to live. Feed your needs. Nourish others. Reap the bounty that life offers. You know people who never did or could. The sad, the lacking, the downtrodden. The complainers who were stuck so deep in their own pain and sob story that they couldn't see daylight if it was about to blind them. And they're gone now. They are either past the point of no return or they've left this life behind.

But you're still here. You're reading this book so you're swimming in a sea of potential. You can be whatever you want to be. It will take some risks and effort, but your life is your canvas. Will the paints you choose be bright or subdued? Will you paint with broad strokes, or refine the smallest details? You get to choose to either stay in the corners or fill your canvas edge to edge. So, what are you going to do with today? Waste it? Let things bubble under the surface and refuse to address them? Remain in relationships or situations that are draining your very life force and making you feel empty and alone? Refuse to reach out for support? Remember: Strength is measured by the courage to get your needs met and to get help when you need it.

Or, will you take responsibility for meeting your needs, adjust your expectations so disappointment isn't your cloak, and put yourself in situations and relationships that allow your needs to be met and allow you to feed the needs of others to your benefit and not your detriment? Will you see that when you and those you care about have their needs fed that the sky is the limit? There is nothing you can conceive of that you can't accomplish when your core needs are met.

You can live intentionally, passionately, and with joy that you've only read about. It's just beyond the doorway you're standing in.

How long are you going to rest there? It's time to claim your stoke, to own your voice, and to be the YOU that you were meant to be. It's time to drop the excuses, put this book down, straighten up, and act on all that you know and feel. In a year's time surrounding the printing of my first book in 2013, both of my parents and a friend of mine died. My parents were both 69 and my friend, Christine, was in her early 40s. I have always appreciated life and its lack of guarantees, but events over the past 18 months have sharpened my resolve to live my life to all its edges and in full color. To not wait for a "someday" that may never appear. I have *today*, this moment, so I'm going to take risks, push the envelope, write it down, say it out loud, and make it happen.

Are you joining me, or are you going to live on the sidelines of your own life? I didn't think so. You've read this book so I know you've got some moxie in you. Let's make things HAPPEN. Don't just *survive* adolescence. THRIVE. And then we can party like rock stars to celebrate. Woot, woot!

> *"I wanna run through the halls of my high school,*
> *I wanna scream at the top of my lungs,*
> *I just found out there's no such thing as the real world,*
> *Just a lie you've got to rise above."*
> *~ John Mayer*

ABOUT THE AUTHOR

"It takes courage to grow up and become who you really are."
~ e. e. Cummings

Dr. Bridget Cooper is an experienced and dynamic educator, facilitator, executive coach, and management and leadership consultant. She was trained in systems theory and uses this orientation to help people of all ages understand and take responsibility for their role in their relationships. Dr. Cooper also received training in non-violent communication, and she encourages you to read Marshall Rosenberg's work on the subject. Her core drive (need!) is to help people to be passionate and invigorated about their lives so that they will propel themselves toward success and create healthy, strong, and happy relationships.

Her talent is developing and delivering interactive and motivational training and keynote speeches on finding your passion and purpose, effective communication, conflict resolution, relationship building, productivity, time management, and decision making and problem solving. She has a proven track record of proactively, strategically, and effectively helping individuals, families, and organizations find peace, inspiration, and happiness.

She has conducted seminars, retreats, and keynotes for numerous associations and organizations including: Girl Scouts of Connecticut, The George Washington University, Bethany College, Manchester Community College, Connecticut Society of Association Executives, L-3 Communications, Glastonbury Chamber of Commerce, Connecticut Boards of Education, Vietnam Veterans of America,

Gateway Financial Partners, Junior League of Washington, Department of Defense, Connecticut Associated Builders & Contractors, Hartford Dental Society, Draeger Medical, USA Weekend, Greater Hartford Women's Conference, Women in Business Summit, B.I.G. (Believe, Inspire, Grow) Connecticut, and American Case Management Association.

Dr. Cooper founded "First Wednesdays," a monthly empowerment workshop for women which brings the lessons of this book to life and creates a forum for discussion and growth. For more information, please visit www.piecesinplace.com.

Raised in New England, she earned her B.S. with a concentration in human resource management from the University of Massachusetts, her M.A. in marriage and family therapy at the University of Connecticut, and her Ed.D. through the educational leadership program at the George Washington University. Her dissertation was on the social network structures of women in academic medicine.

Dr. Cooper has been a leader in the Girl Scout organization, President of the Parent-Teacher Organization, soccer coach, religious education instructor, and elementary school room parent and activity chairperson. Prior to her move to Connecticut, she served as an instructor in conflict resolution and anger management and a motivational guest speaker for inmates of the Fairfax County Adult Detention Center.

Her hobbies include fumbling around on the guitar, traveling to places far and wide, and seeking out photo opportunities of people, places, and things. She has a never-ending bucket list that she's slowly checking off, and she takes suggestions.

Please contact her with your bucket list ideas and information on how she can feed your (and your group or school's) needs at bridget@piecesinplace.com. You can find her at DrBridgetCooper.com or on Facebook (@Bridget Cannon Cooper) and Instagram (#DrBridgetCooper).

DISCUSSION QUESTIONS

"Progress is impossible without change, and those who cannot change their minds cannot change anything." ~ George Bernard Shaw

It takes a village to raise a child, and, well, to do just about anything meaningful. My good friend, Lisa, suggested that I add discussion questions to the back of the book. Why, you ask? Because her amazing teenage daughter, Casey, takes part in church youth group activities and this section would be of great use to youth-focused organizations like yours. So, whether you're a teen reading this so you can chat with your friends about what they learned in this book or what it caused you all to challenge about life, or you're a youth leader who wants to have a deeper discussion with a group of teens, here's your book guide! ☺

There are no cookie-cutter answers. The questions are meant to start a discussion and help you to examine what you've learned in this book and how you'll use what you learned to live a happier and healthier life.

Please feel free to email me if you'd like me to be a guest speaker to facilitate the discussion or if you just want to hear my perspective! If I tell you "I'm cool" that kinda makes it suspect, right? But I am cool. It's true. Just sayin'. ☺

Boundaries & Bubbles:
- How do you keep a safe distance from someone who is a bad influence on you when you see each other in school all the time, or you're related to them?

- What does it feel like to be in a bubble? Have you ever seen anyone model that? What can you do to learn from them?

Peer Pressure & Bullying:
- What are some practical tools that you learned in this book about dealing with peer pressure? Bullying?
- How can you focus on yourself and what you can control and influence when the problem feels like it's coming from the outside and other people are in charge of how you feel?

Romantic Relationships:
- What insights did you gain about having healthy romantic relationships?

Relationships With Your Parents:
- How can you have a good relationship with your parents if they are messed up?
- What is your "job" and what is your parent's "job" during adolescence? What does this mean for your relationship? What can you do to influence it positively?

Teen Violence Prevention Strategies:
- What part do other teens play in teen violence (examples: domestic abuse, peer fights, suicide, homicide)?
- What do unmet needs have to do with teen violence and how can we work to prevent teen violence?

Mental Health and Needs:
- If a person is mentally ill, how do you help them get their needs met?
- How can you keep yourself sane and healthy in the midst of their illness?

Connection to College & Career:

- What did you learn about finding your passion in life and what does this mean to you about what college or career you might pursue?
- How is this affected by what you are "expected" to do?
- If there's a difference, how can you handle it?

Sibling Rivalry:

- Why do siblings tend to fight, aside from just the pressures of living together?
- What did you learn about needs that could help you in your relationship with your sibling(s)?

Peer Leadership & Extracurriculars:

- How do you define "leader?"
- What does "feeding needs" have to do with being a leader of a club or sports team?
- What role do you play as a leader in meeting people's needs?
- How does this responsibility affect your desire to take on a leadership position now or in the future?

Control Buckets:

- Knowing what you now know about "control buckets," how can you manage your relationship with your parents better? Friends? Teachers? Yourself?
- How can you decide when to advocate for something and when to walk away?

Choice:

- What does the author mean when she says that you always have a choice?
- Where/when do you have the hardest time seeing a choice?
- How can you choose who <u>you want</u> to be over who *others expect* you to be? How can you be in charge of defining yourself?

Focus:
- How big of a problem is a lack of strong focus in your life?
- How would your life be different if you had 100% focus on each and every activity (and personal relationship)?
- What would be better? What would be worse?

Stop, Center, Move:
- In what circumstance do you need to practice "stop, center, move" more?
- What does "center" mean to you? How hard is it to get to your "center?"
- What does "intention" mean to you? How can you live with more intention?

Addictions & Eating Disorders:
- What do addictions and eating disorders have to do with our need for control?
- How can we feel in control without resorting to things that hurt us (like chemical addictions, eating disorders, etc.)?

Bottom Line:
- How can we support each other in remembering all of the lessons from this book so that we can use them in our daily lives?

"You can take a picture of something you see, in the future where will I be?
You could climb a ladder up to the sun,
Or you could write a song nobody had sung,
Or do something that's never been done."
~ Coldplay

92941206R00104

Made in the USA
Columbia, SC
08 April 2018